Happy Chri...
Doris

Hope you enjoy
this book.

Love

Wendy & Bruce
xxxx

# FRANCIS KILVERT

Wednesday - 13 - July at 11. a.m. Jubate 76

message which should have been given me
last night. to ask me to go to Belle Vue
to baptize a sick child. I went at once.
The heat was very great. The mother
had just recovered from the measles.
but the child had the complaint still
& cried pitifully & incessantly with
most wearing irritating cry. I cant
think how it is that mothers are not
worn out by the incessant crying of
children. The maternal instinct alone
must be happily very strong to enable
them to go on loving their children
in spite of all they have to endure.
Perhaps that is the very reason. they
love their children all the more for
the trouble they give them. But
that wailing - crying of a sick child
must be terribly wearing. The patience
of women. It is extraordinary. And
happily - for it is all wanted.

A Page from the Diary

# FRANCIS KILVERT

## David Lockwood

*Border Lines Series Editor*
*John Powell Ward*

SEREN BOOKS

SEREN BOOKS is the book imprint of
**Poetry Wales Press Ltd**
Andmar House, Tondu Road
Bridgend, Mid Glamorgan

ISBN 1–85411–032–2
1–85411–033–0 paperback

*The publisher acknowledges the financial support of the
Welsh Arts Council*

Typeset in $10\frac{1}{2}$ point Plantin by Megaron, Cardiff
Printed by Dotesios Printers Ltd, Trowbridge

# Contents

# List of Illustrations

Dedicated to the memory of
Fred Grice
whose conversation and companionship
I still miss: a wonderful friend.

In books lies the *soul* of the whole Past Time; the articulate audible voice of the Past, when the body and material substance of it has altogether vanished like a dream.

Thomas Carlyle. *The Hero as Man of Letters.*

# Series Preface

The Border Country is that region between England and Wales which is upland and lowland, both and neither. Centuries ago kings and barons fought over these Marches without their national allegiance ever being settled. In our own time that eminent borderman Raymond Williams once said, referring to his own childhood, "We talked of 'The English' who were not us, and 'The Welsh' who were not us." Even in our mobile and crowded age, the region retains its mystery.

In cultural terms too the region is as rich and fertile as is its agriculture and soil. The continued success of the Three Choirs Festival and the growth of the border town of Hay as a centre of the secondhand book trade, have both attracted international recognition. The present series of introductory books is offered in the light of such events. We attempt to see writers as diverse as Mary Webb, Raymond Williams and Wilfred Owen in the special light — perhaps that cloudy, golden twilight so characteristic of the region — of their origin in this area or association with it. There are titles too, though fewer, on musicians and painters. The Gloucestershire composers such as Samuel Sebastian Wesley, and painters like David Jones, bear the imprint of border woods, rivers, villages and hills.

How wide is the border? It is two, five or fifteen miles each side of the boundary; it depends on your perspective, on the placing of the nearest towns, and on the terrain itself. It also depends on history. In the time of Offa and after, Hereford itself was a frontier town, and Welsh was spoken there even in the nineteenth century. True border folk of course traditionally did not recognize those from even a few miles away. Today, with greater mobility, the crossing of boundaries is easier, whether for education, marriage, art, or just leisure. For myself, who spent some childhood years in Herefordshire and much of the past ten crossing between England and Wales once a week, I can only say that as you approach the border you feel it. Suddenly you are in that finally elusive terrain, looking from a bare height down on to a plain, or from the lower land up to a gap in the hills, and you want to explore it, maybe not to return.

The elusiveness pertains to the writers and artists too. Did the urbane Elizabeth Barrett Browning, just outside Ledbury till her late twenties, have a border upbringing? Are the 'English pastoral' composers, with names like Parry, Howells and Vaughan Williams, English, or are they indeed Welsh? One wonders whether border country is now suddenly found on the English side of the Severn Bridge, and how far even John Milton's *Comus*, famous for its first production in Ludlow Castle, is in any sense such a work. Then there is the mysterious Uxbridge-born Peggy Ann Whistler, transposed in the 1930s into Margiad Evans to write her visionary novels set near her beloved Ross-on-Wye and which today still retain a magical charm. Further north: could Barbara Pym, born and raised on Oswestry, even remotely be called a border writer? Most people would say that the poet A.E. Housman was far more so, yet he virtually never visited the county after which his chief book of poems, *A Shropshire Lad*, is named. Further north still: there is the village of Chirk on the boundary itself, where R.S. Thomas had his first curacy; there is Gladstone's Hawarden library, just outside Chester; there is intriguingly the Wirral town of Birkenhead, where Wilfred Owen spent his adolescence and where his fellow war poet the Welsh Eisteddfod winner Hed Wynn was awarded his Chair — posthumously.

On the Welsh side the names are different. The mystic Ann Griffith; the metaphysical poet Henry Vaughan; the nineteenth century novelist Arthur Machen; and the remarkable Thomas Olivers of Gregynog, author of the well-known hymn 'Lo he comes with clouds descending.' Those descending clouds . . . ; in border country the scene hangs ovehead, and it is easy to indulge in inaccuracies. Most significant perhaps is the difference of perspective to the two peoples on either side. From England, the border meant the enticement of emptiness, a strange unpopulated land, going up and up into the hills. From Wales, the border meant the road to London, to the university or to employment, whether by droving sheep, or later to the industries of Birmingham and Liverpool.

For the most part, though with one or two exceptions, the books in this series are brief introductory studies of a single person's work. There are no footnotes or indexes. The bibliography lists every main source referred to in the text, and sometimes others, for the use of anyone who would like to pursue the topic further. The authors reflect the diversity of their subjects. Some approach them as specialists or academics, some as poets or musicians themselves, some as ordinary people with however an established reputation of writing imaginatively and directly about what moves them. They are young and old, male and female, Welsh and English, border themselves or from further afield.

To many people the prototype border writer would be the nineteenth century clergyman Francis Kilvert, author of one of the most famous diaries of all time. On the banks of the Wye for many years, Kilvert captured as deeply as anyone has the region's landscape, its people, and his own ecstatic and highly-charged feelings about them. David Lockwood is an authority on Kilvert and a vice-President of the Kilvert Society. Like Kilvert he is an Anglican clergyman, now retired, and lives just two miles from the village of Clyro where Kilvert started and wrote most of his journal.

David Lockwood's three previous collections of poetry demonstrate the quiet sensibility which is needed for the task of treating Kilvert knowledgeably and humanly at once. So does his *Love and Let Go*, a book reprinted twice in the 1970s and which describes the tragic event of the death of one of David Lockwood's daughters in an accident in her childhood. It is a story which Francis Kilvert, as much as anyone, would have understood in its profoundest significance.

David Lockwood divides Kilvert's life into clear stages and keeps a sharp line between what we still do and don't know about that life. In capturing something of Kilvert's passionate mind and remarkable sense of nature, David Lockwood writes not as Kilvert's psychiatrist but as his friend; my own response would be that he is something of a Kilvert himself. Maybe there are rather too few of them left among us.

Finally, I am most grateful to Lady Venables-Llewelyn, President of the Kilvert Society, for consenting to write a foreword to this book.

John Powell Ward

# Foreword

It gives me great pleasure, as President of the Kilvert Society, to welcome the publication of this book, the first complete life of Francis Kilvert.

Since they were first edited and published by William Plomer in 1938–40 the Diaries have been a source of pleasure and inspiration to many, and much research has gone into anything connected with the author. David Lockwood has gathered together many threads and made a coherent story of the life of the diarist and the influences that helped to shape his character and thinking, and as poet, writer, Anglican clergyman and a devotee of the writings of Kilvert, he is well qualified for the task. Whilst not unaware of the small weaknesses he brings out to the full the essential goodness and charm of his character and personality and his gifts as a writer.

I am sure that those already familiar with Kilvert's writings will be fascinated by this book and I hope that others who have not already read the diary will be inspired to do so.

It is, perhaps, not inapropriate that I should send this message from a house where Kilvert was a welcome visitor to his old Vicar and his wife, the Reverend R.L. and Mrs Venables. They were obviously very fond of him and concerned for his wellbeing and I think they would have been very happy to know of this delightful and scholarly account of his life.

Lady Delia Venables Llewelyn

Llysdinam,
Newbridge-on-Wye,
Powys.

# Acknowledgements

Here follows a short list of a few to whom I owe much gratitude. There are many more who receive no mention: they are too numerous, but they are not forgotten. There are excellent lunches recalled and countless cups of tea remembered that prove doors are open and a welcome still awaits in many households exactly as in Kilvert's day.

The Revd. Paul Barnes, who made many introductions for me.

Jackie, his wife, who not only typed my original script but more commendably read my handwriting.

Godfrey C. Davies, Archivist of the Kilvert Society who opened up the treasures of the Society for me.

Meirion W. Davies, who, with his ever helpful staff, showed me their collection of Kilvertiana at the National Library of Wales.

Eugene Fiske and Elizabeth Organ, who constantly helped and encouraged in many ways, allowing me to roam at will alone in Ashbrook House, now the Kilvert Gallery.

Jerry Fryer, the owner of the modern Kilvet portrait.

Alan Halsey for the introduction to Seren Books.

Ken Hutchinson for painting his evocative picture of Kilvert.

Dafydd Ifans, Assistant Keeper of Manuscripts at the National Library of Wales for his kindness in giving me access to the June-July diary of 1870 before its publication.

Diana Lockwood M.R.C.P. for her research into the history of appendicitis.

J.P. Ward, editor of the series, for his encouragement and patience.

Edward J.C. West comes, most unfittingly, last. As Secretary of the Kilvert Society and a friend, he has been an abiding help in every way.

# 1.

# Kilvert And His Diary

To open the pages of Kilvert's Diary is to slip gently and softly into welcoming water. You have entered another element. It is an element of time and of a mind of that particular time. It is mid-Victorian and the mind is that of an observant, energetic, inwardly restless but extremely likeable young clergyman.

Who was he? Kilvert was born in a rectory. In that same rectory he received his first education, for his father kept a school. He was further educated by an uncle in Bath before going up to Wadham College in Oxford. He was ordained, served his father as a curate for a year and then moved to Clyro. This is a small village, two miles from Hay-on-Wye. It was then in Radnorshire, now Powys, and either way in Wales. There Kilvert was curate to the Reverend Richard Lister Venables. It was in this village that he began to write his notable diary which he kept up on his return to his father in Langley Burrell in Wiltshire and again in his own rectory at Bredwardine when he returned to the borderland.

Where does he fit in with the many diarists in English literature? The presidents of this particular league of writing are, of course, Samuel Pepys and John Evelyn. The brothers John and Charles Wesley both kept journals, but they are not set in the quiet rural life as we have come to expect of the English parson. The two most famous clerics are Gilvert White and Parson Woodforde. White's *The Natural History of Selborne* (1789) is a collection of letters to a fellow enthusiast on the wild life and botany of his village. He was a gifted amateur naturalist. Parson Woodforde's journal of 1770 is an entertaining account of a clergyman's life in the eighteenth century, remembered perhaps too much for its emphasis on good eating. There is much else of note. Kilvert is their distant heir. He is, however, much more like Fanny Burney, though the society he

15

depicts is far less exalted. He has her eye for the telling detail, the same deft use of adjectives and talent for reportage.

A closer spiritual ancestor whom in fact he read is Dorothy Wordsworth. The same mountain landscapes excite them both, the same poor wandering people and cottagers. They were both romantics. It is interesting to consider that Wordsworth and his sister seriously thought of settling in Kilvert's border country before the compelling call of their Cumbrian roots prevailed, rightly enough, over the lures of Radnorshire.

Kilvert loved the countryside, especially the Border Country of England and Wales. He loved Wales with a passion that made him think that he had Welsh blood in his veins; and so he did, but it was very distant. Perhaps to be Welsh is not only a matter of birth, or even language, but also a certain temperament; an attunement with mountains and the accountable but also unaccountable mystery of the lonely valleys. All this Kilvert conveys with that particular quality which can hamper an artist and writer; English charm. He so beguiles us that we do not just view but partake in an idyll of a quiet day of burgeoning Spring; summer days of picnics and archery on country house lawns; a world of nostalgic seduction. But look again. He is clear eyed and usually uncensorious, but he pins down the gaping inequalities of his time: the poverty, the injustices and the tyranny in some families, both apparent and hidden.

Frank Kilvert is a Victorian writing about Victorians from their midst. He was capturing the living day, or moments of a day just past, the past important to him. He was like a photographer capturing scenes all around him, not the set posed group but the immediate instant. He was by nature an artist and there is an unconscious design and an instinctive decision of choice.

What makes Kilvert remarkable, even above his great contemporaries Dickens, Hardy, Trollope, George Eliot and Gissing too, is that he was not writing to fight a crusade. He had no desire to expose cruelty or unfairness; he just recorded. Yet sometimes that record might be of grievous injustice, or a horrifying event which he was helpless to alleviate. He was nowhere proving a point, nowhere giving mankind the benefit of his thought and opinions. He was no Titan. He was an ordinary man, an accepter of the order and environment in which he found himself. But he had an extraordinary gift, for he was a vivid and even a passionate writer. He loved life, the natural world of clouds, mountains, women with clear cut features, girls with the spell of innocence, flowers with their remote yet immediate beauty and dappled shadows. Richard Hoggart says that "a sort of love flowed from his finger ends." This is true, and unconsciously Kilvert practised the precept of a fellow mystic, also of the borderland, Thomas Traherne the seventeenth century priest and writer, whose writings had not been discovered by Kilvert's time. Traherne wrote, "you never enjoy the world aright, till you so love the beauty of enjoying it, that you are covetous and earnest to persuade others to enjoy it". That is what Kilvert did and, through the diary, still does.

There is a picture by a contemporary artist, Ken Hutchinson, based upon the only really clear photograph we have of the diarist. It shows Kilvert in his black clerical suit, black bearded, dark eyed, looking to the left. Taking up half the picture are mountains and sky; yet they could be fields and snow, for they seem to be moving and changing and the dark skies repeat the colours of the earth.

This picture entirely captures Kilvert. The landscape is essential and as he regards it so, one feels, it is caught in the retina of his mind ready to be transmuted into words. Yet still all is not said of this picture, for the significance is that Kilvert is not central. He stands to one side. Therein lies a deep well of truth, for he is the least egocentric of all English diarists, and in that as in much else he is unique. He never moans. Indeed, he once declared that "It is a positive luxury to be alive". He left evidence of that luxury, life, which is never all sun or all shadow, and his gravestone bears a prophetic quotation: "He being dead yet speaketh".

Shortly before the Second World War, twenty-two closely written notebooks were delivered to Jonathan Cape, the publishers, by a surviving relative. These were Francis Kilvert's diaries. By good fortune they were placed on the desk of William Plomer, the poet and novelist. Plomer was a man of exceptionally wide experience of the world. He spent his childhood shuttling between England and South Africa. With his first novel *Turbott Wolfe*, about the black and white cultures, he antagonised the ruling powers. Plomer went to Japan where he remained some months, and then returned to England. He became an occasional member of the Bloomsbury Group, but no particular society or class could claim him perpetually. He was too curious about all manifestations of life to confine himself to a narrow field. A director of Jonathan Cape, he continued to write wry, sharply observant and often deeply perceptive poetry, and in 1963 was the recipient of the Queen's Gold Medal for Poetry. He was also a Fellow of the Royal Society of Literature. In his autobiography published in the year of his death, 1973, Plomer said that the Kilvert notebooks could not have fallen into more sympathetic hands. In childhood Plomer had had links with the borderland of England and Wales, and he was fascinated by the Victorian age and particularly its literary clergymen.

Plomer did the work of editing with great tact and skill. He pared the diaries, which in print would have filled nine volumes into three, published in 1938, 1939 and 1940. Their success at that time of such dark political philosophy and evil accompanied by upheaval, was astounding. Such quiet and parochial reflections seemed doomed in such a climate, but the reverse proved true. Against such a backcloth of catastrophe and misery readers turned gratefully to the leisurely depiction of another age. Plomer says memorably: "Against his window the colossal country silence pressed — like wadding, but not too thick to shut out the cry of an occasional owl or the sighing hiss of the rain."

It was a world people wished to remember as the rumble of war came closer to become the shriek, crash and thud of bombs and the crack and crumble of buildings. War drew to a close, but an abridgement of the three volumes was made by Plomer and it still sells. We have to remember, however, that it is but an abridgement of an abridgement.

Many have wondered what the whole diary contained. Nearly all of the manuscript was burnt by Kilvert's niece, Essex Hope, who thought that it was too personal and private. More disturbingly William Plomer himself, in a rash and ever to be regretted moment, threw away the typescript he had retained. Some reading the diary are surprised at Kilvert's frankness about his very natural male sexual appetite, which was always constrained and repressed. This discipline came first from his own deep sense of morality, together with his priestly function and rank. Readers began to conjecture what Plomer had censored.

It was my privilege and delight to know William Plomer well. So well that when he was staying with us in 1972, I questioned him on what had been omitted. He answered very seriously, though with a smile. "Really very little. Passages that were too long and boring, mostly about his work."

I believed him and I still do. The three sections uncut, now published, bear it out. Plomer was hiding nothing, he was not offering us an image of Kilvert, but the real man. He put before us, at Kilvert's worst, a man who could be mawkishly sentimental over young girls and have, at times, a distasteful interest in beatings, murders and suicides. This is the unpleasant side of an otherwise pleasing personality. Fortunately it surfaces rarely and because it surprises it shocks.

William Plomer had a deep veneration for Chekhov. There is a link between the characters of Kilvert and Chekhov. They wrote in different countries, but about very similar people. They lived an equal lifespan of about forty years and they were interested in peasant people and the inhabitants of country houses. V.S. Pritchett has described Chekhov's sexual temperature as low. I would describe Kilvert's as normal, but inflamed at times by unfulfilment. Chekhov, by his profession as a doctor, knew so much more, and living in a more lax society was not so repressed. They shared many interests in the landscape, and they were both amongst the first to be aware of man's responsibility towards it. In this they are both modern and would fit into our own time.

The difference between them is that Chekhov was a professional writer, a genius with a sense of design, a delineator of character and having an amazing ability to say nothing which became something. Kilvert was always the amateur who wished to be a writer. He is, as diarists are, formless. They shared genius, but a different genius.

Since the death of William Plomer, three notebooks have been published, two by the National Library of Wales under the editorship of Dafydd Ifans in 1982 and 1989. Another published in 1989 is the account of Kilvert's Cornish Tour, edited by Richard Maber and Angela Tregoning. So we now have the originals to set beside the Plomer editions.

Plomer's version by skilful punctuation and division makes a slightly more refined and elegant appearance. Blanks to be filled in later by the diarist do not appear. So there is a blander effect, a more fluent articulation. But I can see that Plomer's answer to me was correct; he left out "churchy" bits. Not of doubts and thoughts about belief, but about linen caps for the girls about to be confirmed and the hanging of iron gates for the churchyard. Plomer does, in fact, subtly but also unconsciously, endow Kilvert with something of his own slight Bloomsbury urbanity.

I do know, for instance, from William Plomer's stays with us that he tolerated cats and dogs. He did not love them. Reading the uncensored note books one realizes that Kilvert loved dogs dearly, and there seems scarcely one that he does not comment upon in his visitings. Plomer had not thought this aspect of Kilvert interesting, so he left it out. The same unconscious principle applied to horses, the animal so essential to the mobile Victorian. Kilvert appraises them; a lazy one in Cornwall is called "a slug", but usually it is a word of praise. Also, Kilvert's compassion for the dying horse of the Venables is omitted.

# 2.

# Beginnings

In 1835, three years after the great Reform Bill which changed Parliament and only one year after the near total destruction of the Houses of Parliament by fire, a much more prosaic event took place. Robert Kilvert, future father of the diarist, moved into Hardenhuish Rectory. He had served two curacies, one very happily at Keevil, and another at Melksham where his health broke down. He had encountered disappointment and because of his lack of money everything had been a struggle. But in Hardenhuish, a hamlet on the edge of Chippenham in Wiltshire, he was to enter a period of security and a certain assurance. True, he remained poor, for the living was financially little better than a curacy. However, his patron T. Clutterbuck of Hardenhuish House was generous and understanding and he enlarged the rectory so that Robert Kilvert could take in pupils, as nineteenth century parsons so often did.

In 1838 Robert Kilvert married Thermuthis Coleman, the daughter of Squire Coleman of Kington Langley, a village a few miles away. Her father was a very dark man with a sallow complexion: he also had a very friendly approach to all he met with. So it seems he passed on something of both his looks and his nature to his grandson. Mrs Kilvert's grandparents were Squire and Mrs Ashe of Langley House in Langley Burrell, the adjoining parish. They were imperious people, and Mrs Ashe was generally known as Madam Ashe: both resented the marriage of their daughter to the easygoing Walter Coleman. Thus it was that Robert Kilvert, by marriage, became involved and linked with two landowning families, and one of them had the power and the energy to enforce its wishes.

The Kilvert marriage seems to have been a very happy union. Six children were born of whom Robert Francis Kilvert, the diarist,

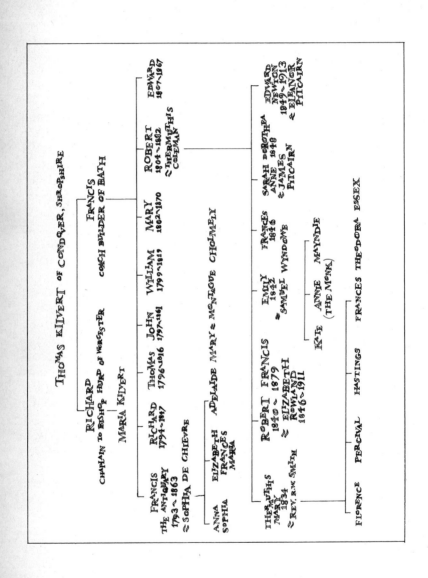

THOMAS KILVERT OF CONDOVER, SHROPSHIRE

RICHARD
CHAPLAIN TO BISHOP HURD OF WORCESTER
= MARIA KILVERT

FRANCIS
COACH BUILDER OF BATH

FRANCIS
THE ANTIQUARY
1793~1863
= SOPHIA DE CHIÈVRE

RICHARD
1794~1847

THOMAS
1796~1816

JOHN
1797~1861
= ADELAIDE MARY = MONTAGUE CHOLMELY

WILLIAM
1799~1819

MARY
1802~1870

ROBERT
1804~1882
= HERMUTH'S COLEMAN

EDWARD
1807~1867

ELIZABETH
FRANCES
MARIA

ANNA
SOPHIA

ROBERT FRANCIS
1840~1879
= ELIZABETH
ROWLAND
1846~1911

EMILY
1842
= SAMUEL WYNDOWE

FRANCES
1846

SARAH DOROTHEA
ANNE 1848
= JAMES
PITCAIRN

EDWARD
NEWTON
1849~1913
= ELEANOR
PITCAIRN

THERMUTH'S
MARY
1834
= REV. R. M. SMITH

KATE ANNE MAYNDIE
(THE MONK)

FLORENCE    PERCIVAL    HASTINGS    FRANCES THEODORA ESSEX

was the second child. However, though the connections on Mrs Kilvert's side were socially a little superior to those of her husband, the talents came almost wholly from the Kilvert side, for they were cultured and cultivated people.

The original family came from Condover in Shropshire. Thomas Kilvert had two sons. One was Richard who was ordained and became chaplain to Bishop Hurd of Worcester, the friend of King George III and Queen Charlotte. He was a favourite at Court and Fanny Burney, then a lady-in-waiting, described his face as the "beauty of holiness". Richard was to become a Canon of Worcester Cathedral and acquire a considerable fortune. It was his daughter's funeral in 1870, attended and recounted by the diarist, which Virginia Woolf was to declare the funniest funeral in English literature. Richard's younger brother, another Francis, was to move to Bath when his father died in 1782. He set up house in Widcombe with his mother and became a coach-builder. This would appear to be a very safe occupation in a city like Bath where the rich and fashionable resorted to gossip, to gamble, to dance, to eat and drink and incidentally to take the waters. Success eluded Francis, and the bank where both his money and his wife's was lodged failed. In 1794 he was declared bankrupt. This misfortune did not prevent his fathering six more children and in all he had eight. According to the *Memoirs* of his son, he was a popular man, very methodical and often called upon for advice in business and to arbitrate in disputes. His greatest love was for sport, duck shooting and fishing. The Kilvert family almost colonised Caroline Buildings in Widcombe. An uncle lived at number 11, Grandmother Kilvert lived at number 15, and Francis and his wife with their numerous family occupied number 7. There was constant movement between the houses.

Caroline Buildings still have charm today, but two hundred years ago it must have been greater. The position remains the same, looking across to the Abbey and the churches and up the hill where the great crescents and terraces still dominate. This is a poorer part of Bath and it looks up to the Circus and the fashionable world. But in its own parish Caroline Buildings had a definite place, superior to the hovels and the cottages which have disappeared. It was a splendid place for boys to grow up in, fields and gardens before them and behind and, then as now, the dangerous but alluring canal with its wonderful system of locks known as the Widcombe Flight. The children enjoyed a free and happy upbringing.

Their grandmother was a very influential figure who had extremely pronounced likes and dislikes. She did not care for her daughter-in-law, or any of her grandchildren with the exception of two, Francis and Robert (father and uncle of the diarist). To these two boys she was both indulgent and severe. One day Robert, a very small child, chose not to go to school. Instead he went to his grandmother's house and lay contentedly on two chairs in the parlour. The grandmother connived in this, but when Robert's truancy was discovered, and his mother and schoolmistress, a Miss Evil, came to carry him away resisting heartily she was unable to rescue him because of her laughter. Every day at five o'clock he had to present himself at her tea table, and every morning after breakfast he had to read her the psalm set for the day. At one time he developed a stammer because he imitated a boy at school, and even though a favourite, every time he stammered he felt the hard wood of the yardstick.

Between the eldest son Francis and Robert were eleven years, and in 1817 father Francis died leaving his six sons and one daughter in the hands of his widow and son Francis. The latter was already at Oxford but he shouldered the burden very efficiently and manfully, and they continued to live in Caroline Buildings. Francis knew that his own career pursued successfully would best help his family. He got his degree, was ordained, and became curate of Claverton. And there in Claverton Lodge, a splendid stone house built by the road and high above the garden which falls sharply down to fields still, he set up his very successful school where his nephew the diarist was to spend the formative years of his life.

This Francis was an historian, an antiquary and a lover of literature. He is the only Kilvert to be included in the *Dictionary of National Biography*. Like all the Kilverts he was a man who put down firm roots and had an intense love of place. He loved Bath, and when he was offered the post of Principal of Queen's College, the combined theological and medical school in Birmingham, he refused it. His love of Bath prevailed and he continued running his school for boys and presiding over literary meetings and dinners there.

He married in 1822 a lady who was as formidable as her names;

Eleanora Adelaide Sophia Leopoldina de Chievre, daughter of Count Leopold van Berthold of Buchlau of Moravia. This gentleman had been sent by Joseph II, Emperor of Austria, to Paris to plead with the revolutionaries for the life of Marie Antionette, sister of the Emperor. He was caught up in the Terror and his daughter, disguised in a fishergirl's clothes, crossed the channel in an open boat. In Dover she was met and befriended by a benevolent Quaker who became her guardian. She lived in his house, Stockwell Park near Clapham in London, until her marriage. She was a figure of awe to children, arrayed in a black wig and always bearing a very stern manner. She wrote a book on the upbringing of the young menacingly entitled *Home Discipline*.

Both Francis and his wife (even now, one does not use any of her christian names), were liked and noted figures in Bath society. Francis, like most of the Kilverts, was the more genial. He was an important influence, first on his brother Robert and then on his nephew the younger, more famous, Francis Kilvert. He taught and trained his younger brother so that he, too, could teach and so supplement the family income. Seeing his brother's worth he interested his more powerful friends in him, especially Stafford Smith, a friend of John Keble who was then a Fellow of Oriel. The result was that Robert was offered an exhibition by thè Provost and went up to Oxford in 1822.

Oriel was the gentle foundry where the catholic basis of the Church of England was hammered out by Keble, Newman, Pusey and Froude in the 1830s and 1840s. Though Robert was an evangelical, it affected him, but much more his son who, like-wise no high churchman, wanted always order, dignity and comeliness in his churches. Robert wrote a record of his own life: it is lively, loving and, like his son's diary, a truthful account. He led a singularly quiet and scholarly life at Oxford, working every morning and evening, and walking for two hours most afternoons. He was very abstemious; amazingly he never drank any alcohol throughout his undergraduate days. Early in life he had an aversion to tobacco which his son inherited. The austerity was not entirely self-inflicted, for much of it was due to his poverty. At that time private tuition had to be paid for, and this unhappily he had to forego. He read omnivorously but without sufficient method or analysis. When it came to his Finals he became confused and exhausted and suffered a minor breakdown. He had aspired to a First but he got a Third: as he put it years later, "to my great disappointment and mortification." It is strange to ruminate that Newman, Matthew Arnold and much later, possibly for different reasons, A.E. Housman suffered much the same fate.

Robert Kilvert became a curate in Keevil, a village near Trowbridge, on the princely sum of £60 per annum. This enabled him to offer a home to his sister and to keep a servant. Then, as seemed natural to his clan, he took in some pupils. He was happy there and considered it very beautiful, but he had to concede to his son, years later, that Clyro was still more beautiful. He remained at Keevil for five years until there was a change of incumbent, and then, as was the custom, the curates left with the vicar so that the new man could appoint his own staff. As mentioned he went to Melksham near Bath, where the work proved too much and it seems he suffered a breakdown. There is then a blank such as his son's life for quite other reasons was to display. Then Mr Clutterbuck offered him the parish of Hardenhuish. The Clutterbucks had lived at Widcombe Manor so they were acquainted with the Kilverts, and they proved good friends. In the manner of the eighteenth, nineteenth and even still in the twentieth century, the church functioned through social contact, even more than most professions.

Secure, with a superb small eighteenth century church and a house which fitted well with it, Robert was able to look for a wife. Thermuthis Coleman was a very capable woman, who, it seems, entered easily into the taxing task of running not only a vicarage but a school, and bearing six children as well. There were altercations. Both Mr and Mrs Kilvert were masterful and servants who disobeyed were dismissed. All allusions to her by her children are affectionate, though it must be mentioned that the bond between the diarist and his father is greater than with his mother. When she stays with him in Clyro and he is invited out to dinner, he does not hesitate to leave her alone; when his father stays he refuses the invitation. We are able to conjure up the life in the rectory very well for Emily, Kilvert's sister younger by two years, wrote of it in her 'Rambling Recollections'. Like her brother she knows the importance of the minor detail to make the narrative vivid. They are the work of an old lady and there is a refrain throughout which charms rather than annoys: "but all this is a digression". She conjures up well the family and the school which seems but an extension of it.

The school had, at first, six pupils who could well be called 'sprigs of the nobility'. The most remarkable pupil was Augustus Hare, who became a celebrated writer. His books of reminiscence and travel, such as *Walks in Rome*, were eagerly sought in the latter part of the century. His memories are harsher than Emily's; for example he described Robert as "hot tempered and [he] slashed our hands with a ruler and our bodies with a cane most unmercifully for exceedingly slight offences." He also says that on his first evening there, "I was impelled to eat Eve's apple quite up — indeed the Tree of Knowledge of Good and Evil was stripped absolutely bare: there were no fruits left to gather".

This shedding of innocence would have occurred at any school, possibly with less promptitude. The headmaster cannot really be blamed, for one prurient boy in a dormitory could often be held responsible. However, his violent means of teaching is to late twentieth century eyes blameworthy. It was the mode of the day and the tradition in which he had been brought up. Kilvert the diarist, for all his intense love of children, also subscribed to the belief that to spare the rod was to spoil the child.

Augustus Hare remembers the monotony of the lessons and the narrow confines of house and yard. This was no doubt just and the rectory must have contrasted unfavourably with his luxurious home and the Italian Palazzi which were a feature of his later life.

Emily remembers that "the boys regularly played in the great field" across the road; cricket, rounders. She also remembers that "one day the boys came back from this field with their jacket pockets and caps full of the most extraordinary chestnut coloured bats, a good deal larger than the ordinary grey ones . . ."; "they let them loose in the large schoolroom where they ran and flew about shrieking to Mama's and the maids' horror."

Was the amiable father a terrifying schoolmaster? Only Kilvert could answer this for the day came when Frank, as he was always called by intimates, "went over to the boys". Did he, one wonders, lose his innocence instantly? He certainly did have some sexual tendencies which were unresolved, but can the school be blamed?

Even allowing for the passage of time to blur the edges of

unpleasantness and soften the sharper memories, the 'Rambling Recollections' summon up a picture, corroborated in the diary of a happy and united family enjoying one another's company at home and on holiday: days by the sea at Dawlish and Teignmouth. It was a full life too. There were outings to the Great Exhibition of 1851 where they saw not only the 'Kohinoor' but the Queen, Prince Albert and several of the royal children. "I remember also Mama remarking how very cross the Queen looked". They went to the zoo and when Frank saw the hippopotamus come dripping out of the water he asked where his bath towel was, which made the onlookers laugh. Was this as naive as his sister suggests, or was it, more likely, Kilvert's desire to amuse people, an early essay into irony? A small boy's humour is sometimes misunderstood.

The school and the family often gathered around the lamps whilst the headmaster-father read to them, or recounted the stories of Sir Walter Scott. They loved listening and he relished reading aloud which he did exceedingly well. Years and years later we learn how he read *Les Miserables* to the family in Langley Burrell.

The household was typical of the growing upper middle classes of Britain, orderly and disciplined but with fun continually breaking through. But there were harshnesses. Emily remembered, evidently with regret and even a sense of guilt, the occasion when the coachman refused to whip the dog 'Dash' saying that the fault lay with the children who encouraged him, rather than the animal. Emily reported this back to her father and the manservant was dismissed. There was another occasion when Mrs Kilvert reproached the cook about the scrubbed table and it was the cook who gave instant notice.

It was this environment that moulded but fortunately did not constrict Kilvert. It explains why when an adult, so good at easy friendly relationships and readily able to cut through the barriers of class distinction, he still sometimes showed a lack of understanding and compassion with servants. Once in Clyro he stormed because the maid let the fire out on a cold day. He referred to her as "a beast". Again in Langley he agreed with the gardener John Couzens, who was being sycophantic to his employers, that the homesick maid who ran away should be whipped. It makes one realize how easily everyone reacts to current conventional notions unless one pauses to think.

Going round the Rectory today one notes the first and second class bedrooms. The servants' rooms face north, and to this day they are cold. The walls are only one thickness of stone and lined with wood and then plastered. The grates are extremely small and the likelihood of their having been lit, except in extreme illness, is slight indeed. One is reminded that the nineteenth century was stratified and that the Kilverts had their place in an ordered society.

Emily mentions revealingly the occasion when they went to an evening party at Hardenhuish House and Captain Hugh Clutterbuck, fairly recently wounded in the Charge of Balaclava, wheeled himself about in a self-propelling chair. Thersie had had her hair dressed especially for the occasion, "a velvet bandeau round her head and a beautiful shaded ribbon bow crimson ribbed pinned behind". Kilvert said "how well she looked, quite fit for a grown up party".

The ever observant Kilvert with a quick and appreciative eye for beauty and elegance was showing his interests. It is good that he was able to express his feelings within the family; there were evidently no repressive ideas of manliness to inhibit him. Here he was fortunate, for later in life the pressure of a more conventional society was to make him keep such feelings for his diary.

It was on the family's return from London and the Crystal Palace, the cross Queen and the wet hippopotamus, that Kilvert was sent to Bath to continue his education. He went to Claverton Lodge, so he did not leave his family, for his headmaster was none other than the kind, courteous mainstay of the family, his uncle — the other Francis Kilvert.

# 3.

# Claverton Lodge

Leaving his mother and sisters in 1851 must have been a wrench for Kilvert. He always enjoyed feminine company. Arriving at Bath station there would have been the long climb up Bathwick Hill. Unlike so many boys off to school for the first time, he knew where he was going and what to expect. If his father was as harsh a pedagogue as Augustus Hare remembers, Kilvert may have been pleased to go, yet people often tend to cling to what they know, however imperfect, rather than launch into the unfamiliar. Kilvert was no exception. By nature he was conservative.

In fact he was singularly fortunate. He left a strict establishment and entered a much quieter, more relaxed, more scholarly regime. He set foot in a larger arena, with Bath and all its fashionable migrants, bringing the ideas, notions and current modes of a still wider world. It was still a very clerical world. Uncle Francis, benign and urbane, was greatly involved with church life. He officiated at St Mary Magdalene's Chapel, he was an evening lecturer at St Mary's Bathwick and was chaplain to the General Hospital. So Kilvert continued to see at close hand a priest at work. His uncle's main source of employment and income was his school.

One wonders if Kilvert, like his mother, gasped in revulsion when the front door was opened and the fumes of the new fangled gas-fire stung their nostrils? He was always a fierce lover of fresh air. Then, like his sister Emily, he was no doubt impressed rather than attracted by the formidable Mrs Kilvert sitting upright in her chair surveying the pupils and all else that came beneath her stare and ardent judgement. She seems a woman who had a far greater need to impress and be revered rather than be loved.

The best source of knowledge about the school comes from one of its pupils, W. Warde Fowler, a very distinguished ornithologist.

Later in life he became Rector of Lincoln College, Oxford. He wrote his *Reminiscences* and in them speaks of his two years at Claverton Lodge as

perhaps the happiest and most fruitful of my life. It was an entirely new life of freedom that my brother and I lived then, and this was true, both of home and school. I will say a word first about the school, for it was in every respect unlike a private school of today. It had been for many years kept by an old fellow by the name of Kilvert, or Gaffer as we called him. He was a scholar and to some extent a man of letters.

His features austere after the fashion of schoolmasters [was] yet kindly and benevolent.

But what I owe most to the school is the entire absence of any pressure of cramming. It is an astonishing fact that I cannot recollect ever doing a written examination in all the two years I was there. I search my memory in vain. I may have had such an experience, but if so it left no impression on my mind either for good or bad. Perhaps we were what would now be called slack. My brother and I played no games, went for no runs, shirked all the work we possibly could; yet I cannot allow that we wasted our time altogether . . . . but what did we do with out time?

In the first place we read all the books we could lay our hands on in the house, and added to them many from the circulating libraries of the city: what they were I do not well remember, but they must have been well-written books for we could, both of us, write quite good English in these same years. I call to witness a single number of a paper we used to produce every week or so called the 'Chatterbox'. The one surviving number opens with an article on the feather of butterflies wings, written by me; another, of my brother's, about some story of Greek mythology. In neither of these is there any failure of English. Then again, we used to explore the whole city of Bath, making the various churches points to aim at — the Roman remains and the Museum we knew, of course, quite well.

It was a place where young minds could open, expand, bloom and, as in the way with schools, fruit elsewhere. Kilvert was no exception and though he writes of the school very little, yet he retained a great love for the city of Bath, always rejoicing in its beauty, in spite of the fact that formal classical architecture, as to most romantic Victorians, was not his idea of beauty. It was insufficiently picturesque.

Kilvert must have read many books; his mind was well-stored with tales of Greece and Rome and here he must have read the great English poets which he knew well (though not thoroughly; he often misquotes). His lessons equally nurtured him in the ancient classics. Kilvert's general knowledge in literary and historical fields was wide and varied. But it was not more so than the average well-educated Victorian. Even the girls, taught for the most part by governesses, were remarkably well informed.

However, the unstructured nature of the teaching, and the lack of practice in examination methods, were to be stumbling blocks for Kilvert. Looking at his writings though, one is thankful that his youthful training had been so free. Kilvert was almost of the last generation of his class not to attend a public school: his younger brother, Edward, went to Marlborough. It is interesting to speculate what a public school might have done to Kilvert. It might, possibly, have made his sexual attitudes more straightforward, but my feeling is that it would have curtailed his natural lyricism and fitted those very English blinkers to his responses. He would have been a more predictable man, a better leader and a much duller character altogether.

Instead, in spite of being to some extent still within the family circle, he was being initiated into a wonderfully liberal attitude to life and learning. He must have felt a bond with his uncle for they had marked similarities, no doubt partly inherited. Both men were by nature considerate and by upbringing well-mannered and courteous: both exercised charm without any effort. Both loved children and equally they had a deep love for the place where they lived. This made them put down roots and form lasting relationships, which made it hard for them to move, and so blunted their ambition.

Uncle Francis left a poem of very personal nature:

*Je Pense Plus*

Though tied my tongue and brief my speech,
Slow to converse, nor apt to teach,
Bad at expounding, worse to preach,
I think the more.

Though backward found at repartee,
My mood constrained, not gay nor free,
Silent and grave midst festive glee,
I think the more.

Though indisposed to speak my mind,
Little to argument inclined,
In range of general lore confined,
I think the more.

Though from religious prate I shrink
Shun controversy as Hell's brink,
Nor with wide ear scandal drink,
I think the more.

Though brave in silence to receive
What friends in glowing kindness give
Nor with loud thanks my heart relieve,
I think the more.

Frederick Grice, a dedicated Kilvert scholar, read me this poem without revealing the name of the author. My immediate question, when he finished, was whether Kilvert had written it. For it enshrines so much of the diarist's character, especially as revealed in the Plomer selections. It is amazing.

It is the poem of a man introverted at the time of writing, but not wholly so, or a poem would not have come, an inner assessment of a man alone. It is the character at the core but not, in fact, as revealed in society by either of these two Francis Kilverts. Often they may have wished to be silent and certainly did not say all they might, but they were good conversationists; both were good teachers and, to judge from his only extant sermon, the diarist was a good preacher, if over-full. The second verse is true, but only in certain moods. The third verse is certainly true of Kilvert. He thoroughly disliked argument because his mind was not academic or critical. The fourth verse speaks openly for both. In religion they were adherents of the Church of England but essentially unconfined and their vision of God was a wide one.

Both of these Kilverts were listened to, indeed were listened to with eagerness: both were welcome at gatherings of all kinds and certainly the diarist could give a smart piece of repartee on occasion. What is said is true of the inner studious man, but neither of them, by their modesty perhaps, were good judges of their social worth. No doubt few of us are. Both were thoughtful men and felt the need to be alone, to ponder and consider or, often in the younger man's case, just to rejoice in the wonders of the world around him.

Undoubtedly the ethos of Claverton Lodge on the young sensitive mind was influential and life-lasting. Kilvert remained a reader of poetry for ever. Even in the nineteenth century, many who loved poetry when young allowed the business of everyday to crowd it out. Some, then as now, seemed to draw a fine distinction between poetry and the Bible, apparently never realizing that so much of the latter is pure poetry. If we compile a list of the poets Kilvert read, it is long and impressive and is not composed of the great poets of the past only. There are contemporary names; Browning, for instance, with whom one does not immediately couple Kilvert. If we then put the array of poets against the list of novelists, the difference is very striking indeed. There is no mention of Dickens, Thackeray, the Brontës, George Eliot, or even the great writers of the eighteenth century, Smollett or Fielding. We do know that he heard Dickens read aloud by his father, and Scott had been a favourite at Hardenhuish. It seems strange too that Kilvert, who so loved history, apparently never read Carlyle who so vividly and energetically lifted the curtains shrouding history.

We can be grateful to Uncle Francis for having a liberal outlook. He helped an artistic mind to develop and be unashamed and uninhibited in recording impressions truthfully. Our debt to this scholarly gentleman cannot be over-estimated, for he enabled his nephew to pursue his own path and inclinations in a society which became increasingly rigid as it progressed through the reign of Queen Victoria. It is easy to think of many schools which would have suppressed and crushed Kilvert's bent. Like so many of his compeers, in his and later generations, he would have become the conventional gentleman with a thick, not necessarily hard, crust over his real emotions, at first masking and then deadening all real and original reactions.

What would it have been like if Robert Kilvert had had sole care of his son's education? It would have meant a more constrained outlook and a vision considerably more parochial. One wonders whether, if Uncle Francis had lived, he would have been more

34

encouraging to Kilvert when he wished to publish his verse? It is doubtful if he could have freed it or improved it, for the soul of Uncle Francis was pre-Wordsworth, pre-Shelley, pre-Keats. Like the city he lived in he was an Augustan.

When the day came for the recessed front door of Claverton Lodge to close behind Kilvert as a pupil, the main mould of his character was formed. He was about to become an undergraduate at Wadham College, Oxford.

# 4.

# Oxford

In June 1859, aged nineteen, Kilvert entered Wadham College. Of his actual time there we know very little, but it was a time of happiness. We can be certain of this for he returned there and he remembers it always with affection. When he revisits the place it is always the gardens and the trees that he finds full of nostalgia, much more than the architecture.

Wadham was the right college for such a countryman. If you go along the Broad leaving what is now Blackwell's bookshop on your left, and turn left at the traffic lights, you enter Parks Road. You begin to have more space about you, there are the Parks with their stretches of grass, the cricket ground and splendid trees. It is a little away from the cluster of colleges at the centre. Wadham College is on the right hand side a little way down. Keble College is further on, but Keble, of course, was not there in Kilvert's day, not being founded until 1870. Wadham would have suited Kilvert not only for its location but because the gardens are not like the more formal arrangements at some colleges. They are "subtly half-wild" as Jan Morris has charmingly described it. Would Kilvert have appreciated that the founder Dorothy Wadham decreed that the library be built over the kitchens so that the books would be kept dry? Years later Kilvert was much bothered at the damp in Langley Burrell Rectory and on one occasion the entire family wiped down the moisture beaded on the pannelling. Sir Christopher Wren, Britain's greatest architect, was an alumnus of the college. Another was William Walsham How, a notable hymn-writer, who in 1878 offered Kilvert the Chaplaincy in Cannes, which after some perturbation he refused.

We first know of Kilvert's feelings for Oxford when he made a return visit in May 1874, whilst he was at Langley Burrell helping his father. He stayed with Mr and Mrs Charles Symonds in

Holywell. They were the parents of a Langley parishioner, Mrs Dallin. Mr Symonds kept a very large livery stable and he owned as many as a hundred horses at a time. When the Prince of Wales, later King Edward VII, was at Christ Church, he hired his horses from Mr Symonds. Kilvert was met at the station by a son of the family, Murray Symonds, and after an early dinner he sprang straightaway into the swim of Oxford life as he had known it.

First there was Evensong at New College where "the afternoon sun streamed glorious through the great west window of the Ante Chapel . . . suddenly the chapel seemed filled with a flood of bright-robed angels." A little later he was on the barge of Queen's College:

> There was the old scene bright and busy which has been going on ever since I left Oxford. The river alive and moving with all sorts of boats, skiffs and canoes. The great crowd moving down the towing path and the meadows on the Oxfordshire side, the barges crowded with University men and ladies, the first gun at Iffley, the puff of white smoke far down the river succeeded after some seconds by the dull report, the 2nd and 3rd guns and soon afterwards the distant roar, growing nearer and louder, of the crowd running with the boats and pouring over the long Bridges, then the sharp nose of the first boat and the white jerseys of the straining crew gliding swiftly round the corner of the bank, the intense excitement, the shouting, the uproar as boat after boat dashed past.

This is wonderful reportage. It is also the writing of someone who knows from of old precisely what was going on at other points of the Cherwell. It is not novel to him, and not just a recounting of what happens before his eyes. It is an informed observer interpreting sights and sounds at the right time.

But a change came. Kilvert continued to visit old haunts during this visit, getting up early but still missing 7.30 Matins at New College, and ending up wandering in Wadham garden.

> All was usual, the copper beech still spread a purple gloom in the corner, the three glorious limes swept their luxuriant foliage upon the sward, the great poplars towered like a steeple, the laburnum showered its golden rain by the quiet cloisters . . . .

> The fabric of the College was unchanged . . . . But all else was
> altered, a change had come over the spirit of the dream. The
> familiar friendly faces had all vanished, some were dead and some
> were out in the world and all had gone away.

A mood of melancholy had seized him, as it often does when we revisit well known places of other periods of our lives. He wants to see a familiar face and so, very characteristically, goes to see George Hawks who had not only been his scout at Wadham but his father's at Oriel forty years before. There was another visit to the river, another exciting race, but the first rapture has gone.

On his last morning he rose early for the Litany in New College Chapel. He walked in Worcester College gardens, but the illusion had departed as his keen eye saw: "Oxford is much altered since I saw it last, old Balliol swept away, New College extending itself into Holywell, a new and beautiful walk planted with elms from Christ Church to the barges, and a new College, Keble red brick relieved with white, which disappoints me at present."

Some think that Kilvert led the austere life that his father had done with very little social activity. This is unlikely, for Kilvert was not as poor as his father had been. Kilvert, too, had a more gregarious nature.

His visits to France, Switzerland and the Rhineland date from this time, and he may even have travelled as far as Sicily. We know too that at some point he was tutor to De Bohun Devereux, a member of the Hereford family who then owned Tregoyd House near Hay, for in November 1871 he refers to Devereux by name, calling him "my old St Leonard's pupil at Thatch Cottage". Tutoring during the long vacation was a common practice for students needing money throughout Europe, met in the pages of novels from Turgenev to Trollope.

One wonders what sports Kilvert engaged in. He was not by nature a sportsman, either of games or the field. His eyes may have prevented his being able to follow the movement of a ball; his disability is very hard to pin-point, distant views he sees perfectly, but sometimes things close at hand were unseen by him, bees at a hive, or a seal swimming close by in the sea. He scored for the cricket team and played football with the boys, but that was for their sake not his own enjoyment. The only sport giving real pleasure was swimming, and of course walking. He must have learned to swim in the canal at Langley Burrell and continued in Bath. At Oxford he would swim in 'Parsons Pleasure' and always unconcernedly naked as was the custom then for males.

Kilvert's subjects at Oxford were Law and Modern History. The Law is a subject which one never connects with Kilvert at all; it is perhaps too dry and unimaginative, allowing little scope for creativity. It is significant indeed that he never mentions it in his diary. Possibly this lack of sympathy with it caused him to leave with an ever poorer degree than his father, a Fourth. History though was a subject that always aroused his interest, and he, like so many clergy of his day and since, revelled in the links found locally with the past, in the buildings, and perhaps even more in the people. He loved living links with the past. The old soldier John Morgan, a veteran of the Peninsular War, was often visited and guided into telling of the days when he served in Spain, for he had seen all the emperors and kings of those times. He had gorier tales to tell of heads that twitched after being decapitated and the ever recurring stories of festivities when the common soldiers met, calling to one another from trenches, and even exchanging food.

Kilvert liked the human, almost tangible areas of history, the links with the past, almost an "Apostolic Succession" a "laying on of hands". He greatly regretted that the jug from which Charles I had drunk when on his march in mid-Wales during the Civil War was broken by being left out in the frost with water in it. Essentially his was a romantic view of history. It is sad that he was at university too soon to have studied English, which as a serious subject, a faculty, was only included later. He would have enjoyed both the literature and the philological side for he relished discovering and recording ancient words used in Radnorshire and elsewhere. He made a list of them which he sent to his good friend Anthony Lawson Mayhew.

However, Oxford was not without literary activity in Kilvert's time if he wanted it, and it can hardly be doubted that he would. Later in life he was always delighted to meet someone from the literary world. Matthew Arnold, who was very influential in the setting-up of English studies at Oxford, was already in the middle of his first tenure as Professor of Poetry (1857-62). It is a chair that has been held over the decades by many well-known poets, currently by Seamus Heaney. Arnold's lectures were poorly attended, yet some of them were to become his most famous. It would be pleasant to think that Kilvert was amongst the few. He must have known Arnold's poem 'The Scholar-Gypsy', which is so evocative of the countryside all around Oxford. It was reprinted for a second time just before Kilvert went up.

One wonders, too, whether Kilvert and his friend Mayhew were present at the famous debate of 1860, held in Oxford, between Bishop Wilberforce and the Thomas Henry Huxley over the theological implications of Charles Darwin's *The Origin of Species*, which had appeared the year before causing such outcry and consternation. One feels the future clerics should have been present. It was generally conceded that Huxley got the better of the debate; but either way it can hardly have escaped Kilvert's notice, though he never mentions it. He does mention, though, Tennyson's *In Memoriam*, published a decade before Darwin but deeply aware of the new natural science, a theme which he in turn was made aware of by his friendship with the theologian F.D. Maurice.

Anthony Mayhew was Kilvert's contemporary at Wadham, and a close and influential friend. He seems to have been the only person who read parts of the diary whilst Kilvert was alive. He had come to stay at Langley Burrell and "wanders about with his books on the lawn and across the Common as far as the beanfield, where he sits upon [the] stile. He has been much entertained by some of my old journals which I gave him to read, more especially by the accounts of my interviews with the three remarkable men, the Solitary of Llanbedr Painscastle, Father Ignatius and William Barnes the Dorsetshire Poet."

As so often with a diary, those closest to the diarist are not described, for they are accepted uncritically as fixtures of life. Mayhew falls into this category. He was a man of some means who held various parishes but returned to Oxford to resume his studies in language. He lived in North Oxford and in 1880 was appointed Chaplain of Wadham. His greatest interest was philology and he became a distinguished scholar on the subject working in collaboration with Professor W.W. Skeat, one of the really eminent names in English studies.

Mayhew wrote many books, but of particular interest to us is his introduction to *English Past and Present* by R. Chenevix-Trench, which Mayhew revised and re-published in 1889. He tells how Chenevix-Trench's book was placed in his hands by his schoolmaster: "I have always looked on the event as an epoch in my life. For it opened my eyes to a new world — the fascinating world of Words. I was made to see that every word had its history and that the history of many of our common everyday words is as eventful and romantic, as full of human interest, as the external history of nations and dynasties." As Frederick Grice tellingly points out, that could have been written by Kilvert. In Mayhew Kilvert found a friend sharing an abiding interest.

Chenevix-Trench is a name that Kilvert would have known, for he published, amongst other works, two which were often reprinted: *Notes on the Parables of Our Lord* and *Notes on the Miracles of Our Lord*. He would also know him as a writer of religious verse. The *Notes* are gracefully written, full of erudition and poetic insight, showing a tremendous breadth of reading. They became known to every clerical household and many churchpeople. Chenevix-Trench, during Kilvert's lifetime, became Dean of Westminster and then Archbishop of Dublin. There is a story of the old man included in the *Oxford Book of Literary Anecdotes* which would have amused Kilvert. The late Archbishop Trench, a man of singularly vague and dreamy habits, resigned the see of Dublin on account of advancing years, and settled in London. He once went back to pay a visit to his successor, Lord Plunkett. Finding himself back again in his old palace, sitting at his old dinner table, and gazing across it at his old wife, he lapsed in memory to the days when he was master of the house, and gently remarked to Mrs Trench, "I am afraid, my love, that we must put this cook down among our failures".

Age never claimed Kilvert, but it claimed poor Mayhew who suffered from senility which cast dark shadows over the last ten years of his life. He died in December 1916 in the Warneford Asylum. It was with Mayhew that Kilvert visited Paris in 1876. There he met, in the party, Elizabeth Rowland, whom he was to marry three years later.

In the same year Kilvert paid another visit to Oxford, staying with the Mayhews. This holiday, also in May, differed from the former. It is just as joyful, but it is lived on the level of scholars and not livery-stable owners. There is a subtle difference in Kilvert too: he is an older man and has suffered in the meantime. On one occasion in the Radcliffe Library where he sheltered from the rain, he became engrossed in a life of Heine. This is a clue to the visit; it is more studious, and having Mayhew as his host he meets more dons. One is Professor Charles Pritchard, the former schoolmaster who put Chenevix-Trench's book into Mayhew's hands at a formative moment. The conversation with Pritchard was long and allusive, and the older man considered a certain sermon an insult to the understanding of the University. Kilvert misread a twinkle in the eye and laughed, only to discover that the sermon he was referring to was not now the offending one, but one of the professor's own!

The two friends went to the Queen's College barge to watch the races. The races receive little mention in the diary for a character intervenes. He had met up with an exact contemporary of his, David Laing, a brilliant but unstable man. Like Kilvert, Laing had read Law and Modern History, but the reaping of his studies yielded him a First. He became a fellow of Corpus and then he changed his name to Cuthbert Shields: he considered himself to be under the special guidance and protection of St. Cuthbert of Durham. Describing when they met on the barge, Kilvert use such adjectives as "excitable" and "defiant". Later the mood changed and Laing became hospitable, asking them to breakfast with him next day.

The breakfast proved "a merry laughing" meal, intimate and full of mutual interests, and it led them to the reading of poetry. Laing read his own poems on the Highlands of Scotland and then some metaphysical verse of the seventeenth century. Kilvert was greatly struck by the melancholy beauty of Bishop Henry King's great obsequy on the death of his wife. Written in 1624, a true poem of its time, it plays with words yet combines pathos with intellect. It is not exactly the poetry we imagine Kilvert would appreciate but there was I believe more judgement in Kilvert than is sometimes realized. The poem also exactly matches the tone of his mental outlook at that time. The man who could appreciate King could also enjoy Heine.

It is a different Kilvert on this second visit to Oxford, and nowhere better illustrated than when we compare the descriptions of the two boat races. One is flashing and bright with youth, the other just as vivid but with detachment. That same evening he achieved an ambition by dining at High Table. The adjectives are "very agreeable" and "exceedingly pleasant". It betokens that the event was a fulfilment but not a rapture.

As Emily missed the irony of the small boy at the Zoo enquiring about the bath towel of the hippopotamus, so I wonder if we miss Kilvert's irony in his recounting the remarks of the prosaic and practical as well as overbearing Mrs Stone. Mrs Stone was a lady with whom Kilvert lunched at Eynsham whilst in Oxford. She declared that her dying husband's words were; "Anne, whatever you do be sure you always job your horses." These words as the dying man entered Eternity so amused Kilvert and the others that they "did not know where to look." It is worthy of Jane Austen. The meaning can be lost on us today, who live in the age of the motor car. To job one's horses meant that one hired them at an agreed annual sum from a stable rather than owning them outright. Putting this final observation alongside King's intensely felt grief in his poem reveals an ironic gulf indeed.

The diary entry for the remainder of his time recounts a memorable visit to St. Barnabas for a very High Church service when the famous Father Stanton preached. Neither the service nor the preacher appealed to Kilvert in any way.

What did those years in Oxford give Kilvert? They imparted to him a certain assurance, which together with his own certainty of his good-breeding, something very important to a Victorian, enabled him to stand alone. Oxford also equipped him with a key to a door, the door to the Anglican church. He must have left Oxford with disappointment at his poor result. He did not however turn to the Church as a last resort. It was much more to continue a rhythm in which he had been nurtured and well prepared. He was following in his father's footsteps: in fact, he followed much more in the footsteps of his uncle.

Oxford had been invaluable and would hold a permanent place in his heart, but it was not as seminal as Claverton Lodge, nor as important and liberating as Clyro was to prove. Kilvert was a man who had to grow intellectually and spiritually, not in a group, but by himself. This was done in the border country, or as his near contemporary Gerard Manley Hopkins was to put it, "in this world of Wales."

# 5.

# Langley Burrell

Kilvert left Oxford in December 1862, returning to Wiltshire to help his father in the parish of Langley Burrell whilst studying for ordination. While he had been at Bath, his parents had made a move, short in distance but momentous in character. Langley Burrell was only a few miles from Hardenhuish on the Swindon road from Chippenham. It gave Robert Kilvert a larger parish, better stipend and a larger, finer rectory.

It is remarkable how, today, the houses connected with the diarist reflect something of the mood of Kilvert's life spent within them all those years ago. The rectory in Hardenhuish, a house matching the elegant church with all the hallmarks of the good proportions of the eighteenth century, is still a peaceful and hospitable place. It is still a place of life; the owners care for it, cherishing every relic of the school and the household of more than a century ago. In the room where Kilvert had his first lessons lives a lady of ninety who still paints exquisite watercolours. Outside on the busy road to Malmesbury traffic streams up and down, an emblem of life, like blood in an artery.

Langley Church to a sensitive man of the nineteenth century must have appeared much superior to the classical precision of Hardenhuish. It was an architecture they tended to call pagan. Langley's church is old and has many historical associations and an undeniable beauty. The main body dates from 1175 A.D. and is built upon Saxon foundations. The south porch is square with a vaulted roof and is one of the finest examples of its kind. It is a place that gives one a sense of continuity, the living fabric of history. It must have pleased the older Kilvert, as it certainly did his son.

The Rectory is a more imposing house than that of Hardenhuish. The architect was probably John Wood the Elder of Bath, whose chief glory and monument is the Circus there. The front has a pediment with a round-headed window placed centrally beneath it with windows set symmetrically on either side: the front door is also central and flanked by windows. It makes for a dignified appearance. Today the house is set in a small wood where, as I approached, the rusty red of a fox's brush was seen disappearing into the undergrowth. The shutters to the windows made the windows look like closed eyes. Brambles rise in waves to break against the walls and a narrow path leads to the steps. This lovely house is a sleeping beauty, solemn, quiet, breathing stilly. This is oddly significant, for though in Kilvert's life the house and garden were full of active lively people, noisy but attractive children, yet it was only the base for Kilvert. It was from here he went to school, Oxford, his travels on the continent, and later to Clyro. The four year period of his curacy here was a mixed time of happiness and frustration. The house in its present aloofness and withdrawal seems to relate something of his inner life at that time.

Mrs Kilvert was surely delighted to have a much larger well-fitted kitchen with a dresser, cupboards and steps leading up to the hatch into the dining room. Her greater joy could well have been the long drawing room, lofty and spacious. It was the house of many Victorian dreams, for it combined the dignity of the previous century with the amenities of the nineteenth, a croquet lawn being amongst them.

This house, set apart across a field within its ring of trees, seemed secure and safe. It was not, however, the original rectory. That too had been largely Georgian and sited by the church and Langley House. Squire Ashe pulled this down in order to leave his own dwelling distant and remain undisturbed by neighbours. This act of demolition occurred when the Kilvert family were coming to Langley. Some have seen this as a snub to them. It is far more likely that it was a long awaited desire of the landlord and was only satisfied when the previous incumbent no longer required the house. Most great landlords wished to be remote and many moved not just a rectory, but entire villages, beyond the gates of their parkland.

And Squire Ashe bought for the Rectory a very fine house, only a little lesser than his own; hardly a rebuff. Indeed, as relations were to be cool and sometimes hostile between the two houses in a manner entirely typical of Victorian village life, especially when there was a family bond between manor and vicarage, it was a blessing for both families that they were entirely separate.

The parish was wide and agricultural with many fine stone houses and farms, and a most notable brewery of superb and no doubt entirely utilitarian structure which also combined fantasy and charm. This sadly was demolished in 1935. Another feature of antiquity and charm is the causeway which Maud Heath had constructed by instructions in her Will of June 1474. This was a raised pathway from Wick Hill beyond East Tytherton to Chippenham. It crossed lowland especially by the Avon where sixty-four brick archways still support the path. Even today one can feel the generosity of the gift. At first one thinks it was made so that the sellers and shoppers could reach the market dry shod and not stand in wet boots the day long. But then one's reliance on our affluence recedes and imagination informs one that, very probably, when life was insecure and larders not full, this gift saved many from starvation. Kilvert, living in an age where poverty was evident, would have appreciated this better than ourselves. So both Kilvert father and son had an abiding place rich in history and often not only intriguing but very beautiful as well. Kilvert was fortunate that he never lived anywhere that was ugly.

So it was that the Kilverts came to this house, with its large pine panelled hall and very elegant staircase with its beautiful banisters which have been described as the best features of the house. The four main rooms downstairs are all panelled and fine shutters can be used to shut out the night. It is to this house that we can imagine him returning from school, from Oxford, from his trips abroad, from Clyro and St Harmon as well as Bredwardine.

Kilvert rarely describes an interior, unless it is a farmhouse kitchen or a cottage, so he reveals little of his immediate surroundings. But the outside, the world where plants grow, trees flourish and animals and birds move, are always described. So in January 1873 we read "To be alone out of doors on a still soft clear moonlit night is to me one of the greatest pleasures that this world can give". And in October of the same year he wrote:

> Golden autumn weather and almost a summer day, one of the perfect days of the summer-tide of sweet St Luke, still and warm and almost cloudless from the early morning when I walked on the

Common between the Lady's Gates and said my prayers in the
fresh sweet morning air, and thanked God for having made the
world so beautiful, while a red squirrel rustled seeking mast
among the dry yellow leaves under the beeches in the avenue, and
the village people crossed the diamond-sparkling common by the
several paths, and the sun shone on the bright tin can of the
whistling milk-boy, and the tender morning mist slanted fairy
blue across the hollows and deep shadows of the elms.

He muses on the imperious Madam Ashe, his great-
grandmother, who drove down the avenue in her large coach.
Then, as now, the gardens would be bright with Michaelmas
daisies and chrysanthemums. It is a village of bright cottage
gardens.

Langley Burrell was a place he loved but which constrained him.
He so loved his family that he never seems to have been critical of
them, but the surge of uninhibited feeling and exultation was learnt
in Clyro away from parents and away from watchful and
disapproving relatives with power to curtail.

When Kilvert gained his degree he returned home, and in 1863
having, we assume, studied under his father and passed his
ordination examinations for the diaconate, he was duly ordained to
his father's parish as a curate. We learn from the register found in
Hardenhuish Rectory that he went a number of Sundays to
conduct morning service at Kington St Michael. He could not, of
course, celebrate Holy Communion until he was ordained a priest
in 1864, in Bristol Cathedral.

When fully ordained it must have been obvious to everyone that
however much he and his father enjoyed one another's company,
Langley Burrell was too restricted a world for a young man. Kilvert
needed experience and much more independence. In this they were
wise, even though for a son to remain his father's curate and only on
his father's death become the incumbent was not unknown. One
parish in Worcestershire was served by one family for many
generations. So the search for a curacy was begun and soon ended
in Clyro. Kilvert took up residence there in 1865.

# 6.

# Clyro

Through friends and relations, as was then the way with the Church, and to a more limited extent even today, appointments were made and introductions forged. The link in the chain between Clyro and Langley Burrell was the Crichton family who had come to live in Wye Cliff, a Georgian house, alas burnt down, overlooking the Wye at one of its most beautiful points. The Crichtons were relatives of the Clutterbucks whom Robert Kilvert had known when he was a curate in Keevil and later came to know better when he was Rector of Hardenhuish.

Kilvert made the journey by train, changing not only trains but stations in Hereford. He then went down to Hay. He must have noticed at once the subtle difference between the landscape of England and Wales. The valleys become steeper, the trees seem darker and there is, at once, more mystery, more drama.

Kilvet was no doubt met by the vicar of Clyro, Richard Lister Venables. Venables was a man of far wider interests and contacts than Kilvert's father. He had married twice. His first wife had been Mary Dalrymple Poltoratzky, the daughter of a Russian General. Venables went to Russia with her for a long visit which resulted in a book called *Domestic Scenes in Russia*, published in 1839. There was a literary strain in the family, for Venables's younger brother George Stovin Venables, a barrister, wrote regularly for the *Saturday Review* and was on easy terms with the great names of the London scene, Tennyson, Thackeray. He also knew Wordsworth, which would particularly have delighted Kilvert.

Venables wrote to his younger brother about the young clergyman he was interviewing. The letter is redolent of the ethos of his class and time.

I have got a young fellow here named Kilvert about the curacy

48

and I believe it is settled. He seems to be a gentleman and I like what I have seen. He is quite young (23) and will not be in Priest's Orders until Christmas. The Bishop of Gloucester and Bristol has agreed to his leaving his present curacy, which is his father's after the Ordination, and from the tone of the Bishop's letter, which he sent me, it is evident that he is respectable. However, he has referred me to a Canon Shirley of Christchurch and I have written to him as a matter of precaution. He is tall with a black beard and moustache. It will be a great satisfaction to have got this matter hopefully settled.

Venables needed a curate, for his other duties were demanding. He had his estate at Llysdinam in Newbridge-on-Wye about twenty miles from Clyro, he was a magistrate and he usually spent some time at his house in London during the Season.

Today when we read his letter we smile at the great emphasis on whether Kilvert was, or was not, a gentleman. He would have been ruffled had he thought the balance was hanging on the negative side, but it was not. Kilvert had romantic and fanciful notions of his ancestry and claimed some who were, in fact, far less ancient or notable than he really owned, particularly on his mother's side. Both vicar and future curate lived in a world codified and stratified by class consciousness.

In January 1865 Kilvert went down to Clyro. He took up residence in the two best rooms in Ty Dulas, now Ashbrook House and the Kilvert Gallery, and kept then by Mrs Chaloner, the widow of a former agent for the Clyro estate.

One wonders how soon it was before he noted the particular quality of the light that pervades the Wye Valley there. The river, which like a shy child turning back to its mother's skirt when ushered into a crowded room, turns and retreats constantly as if loath to leave Wales. This river catches and throws up the light with a radiancy across the wide fields. It is a tendency that the present writer has only experienced in one other place, Compiegne, where the French royal and imperial courts went every September to enjoy that very light.

This light would pour in through the large windows of Ty Dulas and most of all through the vast gothic window over the stairs containing a hundred panes of clear glass. Tradition says that this window came from the church when it was being restored. Local people also tell of the squire's anger when he returned from a lengthy period abroad to find that the agent had built himself, at the squire's expense, so splended a house that he had the panelling, which had come from the church, removed and placed in Clyro Court.

Kilvert, like any young curate, would settle into his lodgings, unpack his books and set up his place for writing. It would almost certainly be by the window looking across the road to the Swan Inn. In that room he must often have sighed, pushed back his chair, stretched out his long legs and examined the ceiling, where the cornice he knew still runs around the room. Looking eastwards and right he would see green fields and the two houses, one of them, then, a notorious ale-house, at the foot of the hill leading to Newchurch which he came to know very well indeed. Here in this room he wrote page upon page of leisurely prose which reflected the life and the light he lived in, a lambency of its very own. Here he was to spin a web into posterity.

This house, Ty Dulas, later Ashbrook House, is now an art gallery named after him. The paintings are contemporary; no false romanticism, it is not a mere essay into nostalgia. It is life as it is, just as the diary mirrors life as it was. Of all the houses connected with him, this is the most active and vivacious and that reflects Kilvert's days there; lively, happy for the most part, and with talent burgeoning. It is a place of unexpected peace, and the noise from the busy road never encroaches. Inside, it is a place of far greater beauty today than Kilvert knew.

Those first weeks he spent getting to know his vicar (a widower), what was expected of him, and the general layout of the parish physically and spiritually. His vicar he found a lonely man, and from Venables' diary — a laconic volume — we find that Kilvert dined with him often and walked great distances with him. After two years Venables married again. His wife was Agnes Minna Pearson, a plump little lady who, like her husband, took to the dark, friendly and even affectionate young curate.

The churches were the parish church in Clyro and the small chapel-of-ease at Bettws high above the Wye Valley with the half-timbered Rhydspence Inn a mile and a half below it, the border to England. Instantly Kilvert threw himself heartily into his work. Possibly commentators in writing and even in sermons have not realized how committed Kilvert was to his work. He lived at a time when there was a dynamic energy humming away in the churches. It was to last, but it diminished slightly before the First World War. After that great watershed the real change came to the whole of British society, yet only slowly, between the wars, did the full realization come that the old world had gone. This affected the church like everything else, for the belief had gone.

Then there was Kilvert's own pastoral work. There were services to prepare, there were churchings and baptisms, weddings and funerals. He was often called, more frequently than a modern clergyman is, to the dying to ease the last hours of the old and sick, or to baptise a weak baby. He had to take note of the poor, and they were many, for the clergyman had access to funds and clothing and blankets. There was also the need for entertainment and the vicar and his family arranged musical evenings and readings in the hall, or the school. Above all there was the visiting; the contact, considered essential, between the pastor and his flock in their own homes. The women were at home, then, both the rich and the poor. There was much to keep them there; cooking for example, and cleaning was a much more cumbersome and laborious task than now. I remember some twenty years ago hearing an old clergyman, a devotee of Kilvert, saying, "People are so foolish, many make out Kilvert to be a saint. He wasn't, he did no more than we all tried to do." There is much truth in that. But it was Kilvert's friendly disposition that appealed to people. Indeed it still does. Many, and especially women, confided in him and he listened. He listened far more than he spoke, for his own listener was to be his diary where he could speak uncritically, without restraint, and remain uncriticised.

He paced his year to the church's year, Advent, Christmas, Epiphany, Lent, Easter and Whitsuntide and the long weeks of Trinity. He revelled in the decoration of the churches for the great festivals with a wholeheartedness that must have been infectious, for it was an outlet for the artist that was always in him.

An easy, almost filial relationship sprang up between Mr Venables and his curate, and through the older man Kilvert was able to meet many interesting and some exalted people he would not have met in Langley. He was asked to the larger houses; the Beavans of Hay Castle, the Crichtons of Wye Cliff, the Baskervilles of Clyro Court, the Morrells of Cae Mawr, the Thomas family of Llanigon, the Haigh Allens of Clifford Priory, the Webbs of Hardwicke and the Dews of Whitney were his principal hosts. Many of these were clergy so there was an ease of understanding. Kilvert proved, as Mr Venables hoped, respectable.

This society could be likened to, and without doubt they saw themselves as, the gentry and landowners of England. But they could also more validly be kinned with the Protestant Ascendancy of Ireland. They were an addition from above implanted on another culture, the Welsh culture which, then, was dormant and repressed. Many Welsh-speaking parents forbade their children to use their native language; they thought it might be a hindrance to their advancement in life. There was a gulf between these people and the native population, and the religion of the natives was on the whole not Anglican but nonconformist.

It was a gulf that Kilvert was aware of and in his natural way he bridged it. It was partly because, though he occupied a place in a higher society, he remained poor, but mostly because he was so very approachable. He was humble in the truest sense of that adjective. He moved in all sections of the community, returning to his rooms in Ty Dulas sometimes having drunk too much, sometimes seeing stars because he had overeaten; but sometimes with a flea which he had picked up in the wretched cottages and hovels he visited. More than once he notes the lice and refrains from sitting down.

But it was not until five years later, on the first day of 1870 and for a reason we do not know, that he picked up his pen and recorded in the embossed imitation leather small black book his recollection of the previous day. The parish he described consisted of two large houses. One was Clyro Court, the home of the Baskervilles. It is a large house of dressed stone built in the Jacobean manner of the eighteen thirties. It has grandeur but little real elegance. The other big house, Cae Mawr, is nearer the village sitting comfortably in the hillside, and is stuccoed with a long verandah running along its southern side looking out towards Hay and the Wye, and beyond that to the Black Mountains. In Kilvert's day it was occupied by Hopewell Morrell and his wife and family. He was a great friend of Kilvert and his equal at walking many miles over the Black Mountains. The next big house, and that is not large, was the vicarage. There were other smaller houses occupied by well-to-do tradesmen like the Anthonys, who still live in the house Kilvert disliked. There were few houses containing the genteel Miss Mattys whom Mrs Gaskell portrays so well in *Cranford*. The nearest approach to such a lady was Miss Bynon of Pentwyn, a remarkable woman who in spite of attending church built a chapel for the poorer chapel folk of the village. This little place of worship still functions regularly. The remainder were cottages in varying states of upkeep. Many remain, picturesque and now improved. The poorer hovels have largely disappeared. Many were places of charm to the eye if not the nostrils, and Kilvert would note, as we do today, the charm of the lichen on the grey stone, sometimes silver, sometimes gold or green, depending on the time of year and the weather. In these houses were the people whom Kilvert served so well and whose company he enjoyed, like Hannah Whitney, described on her death certificate as a pauper. She was shrewd and intelligent and able to appreciate a world beyond her ken. To her Kilvert related his travels and when he told of Pembrokeshire she said, "Dear God, how many strange things there are in the world".

If one had challenged Kilvert as to his most important task, he would answer "teaching the children". He was regular therefore and the headmaster was able to rely upon him, unlike many clergy of the time in their teaching in schools. The lessons he taught were mainly in the Old and New Testaments. He loved telling stories and his audience responded. He was passionately fond of children and he had a deep longing for some of his own — a desire which was to be frustrated.

Frustration was far from being the main note of his Clyro days. They were years of fulfilment in his pupils and his social life. He was often left alone when the Venables were away, so he became used to responsibility. He had a host of friends and he entered into the picnics, dances and archery contests with enthusiasm. He was a vigorous man, as appears in his writing; it takes a lot of discipline and strength to write the long portions each day which he did. In Clyro Kilvert 'came into himself'. He realised his powers and his weaknesses, but did he ever realise that the keynote of his temperament was contentment?

At Ty Dulas he spent many hours. At first his time was spent preparing sermons, lessons and talks, but as time passed he became more adept and confident and these tasks engaged fewer hours. He read a great deal in that pleasant room with the cat Toby nearby. His taste in fiction seems to have been poor, unlike his feeling for poetry. He read Wordsworth and no poet could be read in a more sympathetic setting outside the Lake District itself. Here were the mountains, the valleys, and the hills of running water, perpetually rushing, swift but like slow music, each stream having its own particular note, something Traherne had noticed two centuries before. And there were the sheep and the people who kept and tended them. Kilvert knew the counterparts of the characters of the *Lyrical Ballads*. He encountered the vagrants that William and Dorothy Wordsworth wrote about so often.

Kilvert's joy in the countryside would have been apparent without Wordsworth. But knowing so much of that poetry made him see with his eye and it heightened his appreciation. On those long walks visiting parishioners in the hills which rise so suddenly from Clyro to the west and which bring one to vast tracts of awe-inspiring loneliness, Kilvert gave his heart unstintingly. But first he gave it to the people, for it was his vocation to love as Christ had loved. It was also his nature and in this he was far more generous and far less egocentric than Wordsworth.

These years saw Kilvert mature, and when he begins the diary we can see that there are two Frank Kilverts. One was sociable and gregarious, and liked being asked out to dinners and croquet parties with all their chattering encounters and bantering humour. We can also see however, that he never wanted too much. One summer there is a perceptible sigh as he recounts yet another social event, but then his spirit rises as he remembers the enjoyment. The other side was the walker who rejoiced "in not meeting a single person, always a great triumph to me and a subject of warm self-congratulation for I have a peculiar liking for a deserted road."

This is, in fact, the poet in him needing quiet. It is also, though, a feeling many country clergy seem to have, a sudden desire for anonymity. They are marked men in a small community, living up to a role of benevolence dictated for them, not just by their faith, which is bearable, but the expectations of others which are unfathomable. There is sometimes an overwhelming desire to escape, to be alone, to be oneself.

# 7.

# The Countryside and Wordsworth

Fair seed time had my soul, and I grew up by land
Fostered alike by beauty and by fear

This is Wordsworth describing his childhood. Frederick Grice invented the pertinent phrase that in Clyro Kilvert "lived in a Wordworthian dream." It is true and in many respects it had much to do with the particular moment of time. Kilvert lived just before the agricultural depression which impoverished the farmers and their workers and the countryside: he lived, also just before machinery really took over the work of the labourer. There were steam engines, but they were largely confined to threshing. It was the same countryside of many generations almost unchanged. It was the countryside Wordsworth also knew.

But it was Kilvert's response to lonely places that brought him close to Wordsworth. The diarist had only to walk up the Painscastle road from his lodgings to bring him to the great stretch of the Radnor Forest where line upon line of hills and hidden valleys stretch; the poet Ruth Bidgood's "multiple horizons of Wales". He loved the emptiness, the mystery, where heaven and earth seem to meet. He wrote: "I like wandering about these lonely, waste and ruined places. There dwells among them a spirit of quiet and gentle melancholy more congenial and akin to my own spirit than full life and gaiety and noise."

This was an essential part of Kilvert the diarist, the reflective, the man who entered into the world of nature. It was the quietist and the artist in him. The word-pictures which he draws are better than the pictures he often admired; to gain a mention in his diary most pictures have to 'tell a story', and in that he was characteristically Victorian. One day in March 1871 he viewed rolling masses of vapour on the Black Mountains:

> This cloud grew more white and dazzling every moment, till a clearer burst of sunlight scattered the mists and revealed the truth. This brilliant white cloud that I had been looking and wondering at was the mountain in snow . . . a long rampant line of dazzling glittering snow as no fuller on earth can white them. I stood rooted to the ground, struck with amazement and overwhelmed at the extraordinary splendour of this marvellous spectacle. I never saw anything to equal it, I think, even among the high Alps. One's first involuntary thought in the presence of these magnificent sights is to lift up the heart to God and humbly thank Him for having made the earth so beautiful. An intense glare of primrose light streamed from the west deepening into rose and crimson. There was not a flake of snow anywhere but on the mountains and they stood up, the great white range rising high into the blue sky, while all the rest of the world at their feet lay ruddy rosy brown.

A man came by on a cart horse. Kilvert in his ecstasy wanted to point the scene out to him, but thought he might be considered mad. This is a moment shared by Wordsworth in 'Peter Bell':

> A primrose by a river's brim
> A Yellow primrose was to him,
> And it was nothing more.

What does all this tell us about why Kilvert kept a diary? There was so much in a life he found so rich that he was unable to communicate to those around him. It was not just the labourers, the farmers deadened by toil; it was also his peers. The Beavans, the Crichtons, even the Venables, were all enclosed in that thin carapace of conventional respectability. Most would have listened but the corners of their mouths would have turned down in a wry smile. It is as though Kilvert, rather more than Wordsworth, made a truce with society. In his role as a priest he had to.

It is all so evident when he was asked to join a rook shoot. He accompanies them, and even admires a man called Trevellyn:

> He is a capital shot. He shot a rabbit with his beautiful little rook-rifle like a long saloon pistol. The old rooks were all scared

away, sailing round at an immense height in the blue sky, and it was pitiable to see the young rooks bewildered, wheeling and fluttering helplessly from tree to tree, and perching, only to be tumbled bleeding with a dull thud into the deep nettle beds below by the ceaseless and relentless crack crack of the beautiful cruel little rifles, or to see them stagger after the shot, hold on as long as possible and then, weak from loss of blood, stumble from their perch, and flutter down, catching at every bough, and perhaps run along the ground terrified and bewildered, in the agonies of a broken wing. It may not be cruel, but I don't think I could ever be a sportsman. It seemed dreadful to bring death and misery into such a sunny lovely scene, among helpless the innocent unsuspecting birds, when everything else was glad and rejoicing, merely for the sake of sport.

Kilvert shares Wordsworth's tension; he can appreciate the beauty of a well-made rifle. He can like the marksmen. He knew very well from his father and brother, both fishermen, that the hunter is paradoxically often the naturalist. Yet we should note that we have his reactions, not his thoughts, which is where he differs from the poet. Kilvert never launches into theories, or any abstract thought. There is, too, a poetic justice in the fact that the shooting party is but an assembly of names. Kilvert the onlooker is the only one known.

He preferred the countryside by himself. He hated crowds. In 1871 he was asked to join the Woolhope Club, a distinguished archaeological society, to investigate a tumulus on the Black Mountain. He refused to go, but urged by a friend, went alone.

Imagine my delight to find the place perfectly silent and solitary except for the sheep . . . . A man can hardly be a beast or a fool alone on a great mountain. There is no company like the grand solemn beautiful hills. They fascinate and grow upon us and one had a feeling and a love for them which one has for nothing else. I don't wonder that our Saviour went out into a mountain to pray and continued all night in praying to God *there*.

The truly memorable and significant moments of his spiritual life were in lonely places, usually alone. For example, when he climbed Cader Idris, one of the most spell-binding and rigorous of British mountains, with old Pugh the guide, he was moved. He wrote of it at length and particularly of the death of Smith, a solicitor's clerk there. He was found "a skeleton in clothes. The foxes and ravens had eaten him". For most of the time one feels that Pugh had come between the mountain and Kilvert, but for a moment in swirling mist, he wrote: "It is an awful place in a storm. I thought of Moses on Sinai". This entry is a delightful mixture of the Wordsworthian and the purely earthly, for as they re-entered Dolgelly the guide said: "'You're a splended walker, Sir', a compliment which procured him a glass of brandy and water."

Perhaps the most magnificent passage which is Old Testament and pagan, which the poet would have completely understood, is 'An angel-satyr walks these hills'. What does it mean? It has a mystic quality. William Plomer, one of the first to read those words, was struck by them and wrote a memorable poem upon them:

> An angel satyr walks these hills,
>     But only to be seen by those,
> Whose fitness he divinely knows,
> To hear the vision and receive the seed
> The child, the virgin, and the wise,
>     Each in need
> To be touched by his life-giving hand
> And to look at his deathless eyes.
> . . . . . . . .
>
> I am love in a perfect form. I show, not offer you, perfection
> That you may take heart again, escape
> Sterilities of knowing, and in the veins the dull infection
> Of prudence seeping. Before you, I stand and shine,
> Earth's essence — therefore, sir, divine.

The Wordsworthian ideal grew in Kilvert and it received two great boosts during his time in Clyro, for he became friendly with the Dew family who lived in Whitney Rectory, a village in Herefordshire, four miles east of Clyro. The vicar, Henry Dew, had married Mary Monkhouse, whose father was a first cousin of Mary Hutchinson who became the wife of Wordsworth. Mrs Dew treasured and showed to Kilvert a sonnet by the poet entitled, 'The Infant, M . . . . . M . . . .'

Kilvert was very impressed and marked the sonnet in his copy of the *Collected Poems*. It is a highly uncritical portrait of a child, and to our eyes sentimental. "The child has no fretful temper", she is "prompt, lively, self-sufficing and meek". She is, indeed, like the Virgin, "Beneath some shady palm of Galilee". A little coyly Mrs Dew admitted that the child was herself. Facts tell a rather different story.

Mary's childhood cannot have been easy for her parents were not happily married. Her father was for long periods ill and her mother, like many leisured ladies of that time, also took to her sofa. When her husband began to sink, her spirits rose and his death was astonishingly beneficial to her health and vitality. Two years later she remarried but died of typhus in 1834. Mary, a backward child, spent much of her childhood at Rydal Mount in the Lake District with the Wordsworths, in Herefordshire with the Hutchinsons at Brinsop Court, and again with her uncle John Monkhouse in Whitney. It was an unsettled and disjointed upbringing with no real home and it must have made her insecure. However, financially she was extremely wealthy, an heiress with £20,000.

She became engaged to Wordsworth's son in 1843. Later she broke off this engagement which incurred the wrath of the poet who with that curious egocentricity of his pronounced her demented. Her next engagement was to a Queen's Messenger. This was also terminated when she discovered it was not her person he desired but her purse. Shortly after this she married Henry Dew who had been rector of Whitney for two years and there they spent the remainder of their lives. Mrs Dew died in 1900 aged 78 and her husband in 1901 aged 82.

Relations with the poet's family had long been restored. In 1871 Kilvert was invited to the rectory to meet Elizabeth Hutchinson, a niece of Mrs Wordsworth and god-daughter of Dorothy Wordsworth, in whom Kilvert was equally interested. They talked of the family, and she showed him a brooch containing a photograph of Haydon's picture commemorating the poet's seventieth birthday when he climbed Helvellyn. She told him much about Wordsworth's character. "He did not care much for society and preferred the society of women to that of men. With men he was often reserved."

The romantic Kilvert possibly thought that his own character echoed the poet's. In fact he was friendly and at ease with either sex. They talked also of Dorothy and again, erroneously, Dorothy's mental decline was blamed upon the long walks. It was a rewarding conversation and later Kilvert received from Elizabeth Hutchinson a manuscript poem of Dorothy's. "A relic very precious to me" wrote Kilvert.

Yet another link with Wordsworth came to him through George Stovin Venables, brother of his vicar. George was a noted barrister and a respected critic of current literature. Whilst staying at Llysdinam Hall the two men went for a walk. Kilvert discovered that Venables had stayed with the poet at Rydal Mount and also met Mary his wife and Dorothy, who was already fading. She "took no part in the conversation and no notice of what was passing".

Venables told him how Wordsworth had met the man who became 'Peter Bell' on the road between Builth and Rhayader, a road known well to Kilvert. A sharper light was thrown on Wordsworth though by the following anecdote:

> One evening riding near Rydal I saw Wordsworth sauntering towards me wearing a shade over his eyes, which were weak, and crooning out aloud some lines of a poem which he was composing. I stopped to avoid splashing him and apologised for having intruded upon him. He said 'I am glad I met you for I want to consult you about some lines I am composing in which I want to make the shadow of Etna fall across Syracuse, the mountain being 40 miles from the city. Would this be possible?' I replied there was nothing in the distance to prevent the shadow of the mountain falling across the city. The only difficulty was that Etna is exactly north of Syracuse. 'Surely' said Wordsworth, 'it is a little N.E. or N.W.' As he was evidently determined to make the shadow fall the way he wanted it I did not contradict him. Wordsworth was a very remarkable looking man. He looked like an old shepherd, with rough rugged weather beaten face, but his features were fine and high cut. He was a grand man. He had a perfectly independent mind and cared for no one else's opinion. I called upon him afterwards at the Stow, Whitney. He was very kind to me there. He used to say that the Wye above Hay was the finest place of scenery in South Britain, i.e. everything south of himself.

Kilvert loved these almost tangible links with the poet. But it was his own swift and constant reaction to the lush lanes and bleak uplands that really connect him with Wordsworth, and his respect for people, those stoic people of remote farms and places. But it was also his manner of life, it bore many resemblances to the poet's. There was a kinship of activities. Being countrymen their seasonal activities tallied. Kilvert went nutting with a host of children. He wrote and illustrated a doggerel report of the occasion. It is another version, but on quite another plane to Wordsworth's gentle, slightly humorous account of his nutting expedition when a schoolboy. Anne Tyson, his motherly land-lady made him wear old clothes and he describes himself:

> a Figure quaint,
> Tricked out in proud disguise of Beggar's weeds
> Put on for the occasion, by advice
> And exhortation of my frugal Dame

Skating, too, was for neither of them the circus round in a modern rink, but the charged atmosphere of a changed world when liquids are suddenly solid. There is magic and this magic is more than apparent for Wordsworth in the setting of Windermere where:

> every icy crag
> Tinkled like iron, while the distant hills
> Into the tumult sent an alien sound
> Of melancholy,

and of his own prowess in skating, he writes that he went so fast:

> all the shadowy banks, on either side,
> Came sweeping through the darkness, spinning still
> The rapid line of motion.

Kilvert's long skating party, days on end, at Draycot Park, is more prosaic and in true Victorian style, the classes are stratified. There is a list of titles, "it was a distinguished company". Some readers have foundered at this point. They have been annoyed by one remark, "I had the honour of being knocked down by Lord Royston." Kilvert knew very well that being tumbled by the poorest beggar is just as uncomfortable as being overturned by a peer: it was his ironical humour appearing and being misinterpreted, just like his remark about the hippopotamus at London Zoo lacking a bath-towel, when he was a small boy. Kilvert's skating is sociological, Wordsworth's is sublime. It gave us a picture to revere for ever; "To cut across the image of a star."

The link between the poet and the diarist went even deeper than this. Both were of a mystical nature, the world, in Wordsworth's phrase, "getting and spending" often appalled them. They received from nature their religion, even the parson Kilvert. It is very unlikely that the sonnet beginning, "The world is too much with us; late and soon", which continues to the climax:

> Great God! I'd rather be
> A Pagan suckled in a creed outworn;
> So might I, standing on this pleasant lea,
> Have glimpses that would make me less forlorn;
> Have sight of Proteus coming from the sea;
> Or hear old Triton blow his wreathed horn.

would have perturbed Kilvert at all. The visionary that wrote of the Angel-Satyr on the hills would have completely comprehended. Once again it almost makes one grieve that neither Wordsworth, nor Kilvert were able to read the other mystic of the Border country, Traherne, who wrote that, "You never enjoy the world aright, till the Sea itself floweth in your veins, till you are clothed with the heavens, and crowned with the stars."

# 8.

# More Countryside, More People

S ome of Kilvert's descriptions of the landscape were memories of scenes he saw from the train. He used the railway constantly, for local journeys to see friends like the Dews at Whitney, or to return home to Langley Burrell. From there he went often up to London, or to Bristol. He paints a picture that makes one thirsty, of the Wiltshire Downs in a drought on a journey to the Isle of Wight. Some see in this evidence of restlessness. I see it more as evidence of a lively curiosity, and with the new and quick means of travel he was able to satisfy it. If his restlessness had been born of depression he would not, I think, have given us such vivid pictures conjured from fleeting glances which have an almost pre-Raphaelite comprehension for detail. In the late twentieth century we drive in cars where he journeyed by railway; we see, as he did along the Dulas valley, the bare uplands, the grandeur, the remoteness of some farmhouses, and we see the bare uplands dotted with sheep and the tops of trees in the clefts below. But few of us write:

> Soon after we left Neath we crossed and recrossed the beautiful Dulas winding through a lovely valley among gorgeous woods. Then we came into a bare region of mountain and deep desolate valleys, with waterfalls leaping down the steep hill sides. The mountains loomed in gloomy grandeur, dark, grey, indigo and purple under a heady cloudy sky. As we drew near Brecon again we got into a beautiful rich woodland country highly cultivated, with lovely dingles and deep green meadows, and a fine gleam of sunshine at sunset lit the dingles and hill slopes and set the gorgeous woods aflame.

Here he achieves by subtle alliteration and assonance a beauty he hardly ever achieved in his poetry. These spontaneous outbursts in his journal were his true metier. On another occasion he described the ever present, ever changing Black Mountains as: "striped and streaked with snow" a sight very familiar to me and my family in the spring when we sit in the scent of wallflowers and look up to winter whiteness.

There was, near Clyro, one place he loved beyond all else, Cwmgwanon Wood. He walked there often, not just to contemplate but on his way to visit the farms where separately lived two women driven to madness by depression. He loved the woods and wrote like Chekhov's Dr Astrov when he heard the news: "the whole of the beautiful Cwmgwanon woods are to be felled, the Castle wood and all that exquisite wooded bank up the dingle to the 'tufted copse' and Bryn y garth. The trees have been doomed, measured and numbered. The sale is to take place next week. And then the axe will be heard in the sacred dingle."

It is, perhaps, because of the realism of the diary that Kilvert avoids the sentimentality that creeps into his poetry. He sees the woods and fields as they are and he links them with the people who live there; and never better than when he records his visit to Mrs Watkins in 1871, on the last day of August:

Her son was out in the harvest field carrying oats, and I had to wait till he came in to go upstairs with me. While I waited in the kitchen the low deep voice upstairs began calling 'Murder! John Lloyd! John Lloyd! Murder!' They sent up into the oatfield for her son, but I had waited nearly an hour before the oatladen waggon came creaking and swaying and sweeping the hedge along the edge of a brow high above the house and then down a steep rough path into the rick yard. The womenfolk of the house were unloading the oats, as their 'harvest man' Griffiths of Tylyhilog had gone off on a drinking bout and had left them in the lurch.

The madwoman's son, a burly tall good-humoured man with a pleasant face, came to the garden gate and thought I could not do any good by seeing his mother. So I went away. But when I had got half way down the meadow Cwmside on my way to the Burnt House he shouted to me to come back and asked me to go up and see her. He led the way up the broad oak staircase into a fetid room darkened. The window was blocked up with stools and chairs to prevent the poor mad creature from throwing herself out. She had broken all the window glass and all the crockery. There was nothing in the room but her bed and a chair. She lay with a blanket over her head. When her son turned the blanket down I was almost frightened. It was a mad skeleton with such a wild scared animal's face as I never saw before. Her dark hair was tossed weird and unkempt, and she stared at me like a wild beast. But she began directly to talk rationally though her mind wandered at moments. I tried to bring some serious thoughts back to her mind. 'Whom do you pray to when you say your prayers?' 'Mr Venables'. It was a dim lingering idea of someone in authority. I repeated the Lord's Prayer and the old familiar words seemed to come back to her by degrees till she could say it alone. When I went away she besought me earnestly to come again. 'You'll promise to come again now. You'll pomise', she said eagerly.

How tellingly that is described, how splendidly he leaves darkened to the end of the sentence — a fetid room darkened. It tells us much about Kilvert and the pace of life. Few people would wait an hour on a visit, and even then he is sent away, but Kilvert's calm worked on the reluctant son, ashamed of his mother's madness, and he is called back. And then Kilvert really makes contact and she asks him to return. He did.

These people are a part and co-creation of the countryside; they are the people of whom Wordsworth writes, but none more so than the Solitary. This man, vicar of Painscastle near Clyro, was a source of some amusement and some amazement. Kilvert must often have heard of him. One day he went up to Painscastle to find him with his good friend Tom Williams, vicar of Llowes. Williams rode his pony and Kilvert strode on foot. After the long climb and dallying talking to the 'Mayor' they came upon:

a little hollow, a recess in the hills at the foot of Llanbedr Hill, a little cwm running back into the mountain . . . a little grey hut. It was built of rough dry stone without mortar and the thatch was thin and broken.

[Inside] was a wild confusion of litter and rubbish almost choking and filling up all available space. The floor had once been of stone but was covered thick and deep with an accumulation of the dirt and peat dust of years. The furniture consisted of two wooden saddle-seated chairs polished smooth by the friction of continual sessions, and one of them without a back. A four-legged dressing table littered with broken bread and meat, crumbs, dirty knives and forks, glasses, plates, cups and saucers in squalid hugger-mugger confusion. No table cloth. No grate. The hearth foul with cold peat ashes, broken bricks and dust, under the great wide open chimney through which stole down a faint ghastly sickly light. In heaps and piles upon the floor were old books, large Bibles, commentaries, old fashioned religious disputations, C.M.S. Reports and odd books of all sorts, Luther on the Galatians etc.

Amid all this Kilvert notes the Solitary's "perfect courtesy and the natural simplicity of the highest breeding". He was moved with compassion: "To be ill and to grow old in that lone hut without a soul to care for him or to turn his head. How wretched a prospect for the poor Solitary".

John Price, the Solitary, scholar of Queen's College, Cambridge, lived longer than Kilvert, surviving a life of privation and eccentricity. He had come to Llanbedr, Painscastle, an exceedingly sparsely populated parish, in 1859. There were few churchmen, few dissenters, and no vicarage. The Church was in ruins in which it remained during his incumbency, but it was used. His vicarage, a hovel, was extended by three old bathing machines, which he had transported from Aberystwyth; one a study, another a bedroom and the third his kitchen.

He held services and a Sunday school. Hope, like his piety, seems not to have flickered. However, even his faith must have been daunted, so he encouraged the tramps to attend and even paid them for their presence, always hoping to turn their hearts. When they complained of the cold he bought oil stoves and placed them between the pews, and very swiftly it was discovered by the vagrants that bacon could be fried whilst the sermon was preached! He was also disturbed to find that many of his couples lived in a union unblessed by the church. He promised five shillings to every couple who submitted to holy wedlock. Some found this a profitable way to gain money and were married under several names to the same partner.

John Price lived until 1895. He had no person close at hand to care for him, but he was watched over from a distance. It was his teasing humorous friend the vicar of Llyswen who called and was alarmed at the old man's appearance. He returned with a doctor and they carried him to clean lodgings in Talgarth where a bath was prescribed. With the utmost difficulty his underclothes were cut away. Washed and clean he was put to bed, beaming benedictions on all for this great kindness and wondering what he had done in life to merit such attention. He slept soundly and never woke. He is buried by the church to which he was so devoted.

Kilvert was moved by this man. It was comparable to being in the presence of an early primitive Christian, or an early follower of St Francis. His like may still be found amongst the anchorites on Mount Athos, rapt, convinced, possibly a little mad. The diarist must have felt too that it was a Wordsworthian encounter. John Price echoed the Wanderer of *The Excursion*:

> . . . . a Man of reverend age,
> But stout and hale, for travel unimpaired
> There was he seen upon the cottage-bench,
> Recumbent in the shade, as if asleep;
> An iron-pointed staff lay at his side.
>
> Strongest minds
> Are often those of whom the noisy world
> Hears least; else surely this Man had not left
> His graces unrevealed and unproclaimed.
> But, as the mind was filled with inward light,
> So not without distinction had he lived,
> Beloved and honoured — far as he was Known.

When Kilvert and Tom Williams left they were aware that they had been in the presence of someone "truly touched by God", and as they were seen along their path by the long bearded unkempt figure Kilvert wrote: "The people who met him touched their hats to his reverence with great respect. They recognised him as a very holy man and if the Solitary had lived a thousand years ago he would have been revered as a hermit and perhaps canonised as a Saint." The often urbane, usually sophisticated William Plomer speaking of the Solitary in the setting of a barn in 1967 was equally moved.

When we ponder the affinity of Wordsworth and Kilvert in spirit and awareness it is valuable to note their difference in literary expression. When Kilvert wrote the age of realism had arrived. Dickens, Kingsley, Victor Hugo and George Eliot had prepared the ground for him. Hence the rich multitudinousness of the muddle in the hovel. Kilvert consciously piles the images to make a magnificently effective picture that tells us so much of the Solitary.

Kilvert caught him in his web. A statement once made to the present writer and only turned into a question for the sake of politeness was: "Kilvert was a loner, wasn't he?" No, Kilvert was not a loner. As a parish priest he knew the importance and necessity for most to be social creatures, dependent on one another, and stimulated by them into becoming full beings. He was not a profound man, he deduced no philosophical theories for mankind. He was a practical man who hoped to show his faith and his beliefs by his mode of life. He enjoyed so many things, parties, company, or the sight of a great port like Liverpool or Bristol. He was able to suddenly stand aside, and view these things and the world objectively. He was in the world that he appreciated but which rarely seduced him. He saw very clearly the difference between Bath and Bristol: "It is a grand city. How much grander than Bath. I breathe freely here. Here is life, movement and work instead of the foolish drawl and idle lounge."

He admired the courage and stoicism of the poor of his day and he was interested particularly in the people in the lonely farms and those unable to make real contact like the idiot child Mary Price of Bredwardine and her patient, faithful stepmother. His sympathy sprang from a feeling of identification with them. For they were often unable to express their thoughts, and Kilvert in the conventional world was unable to express his innermost self too. His real contact had to be in the bright pages of his diary where no judgement, at least in his lifetime, would be made.

If Kilvert were to return today, he would recognise the same stoic people and some of the same loneliness. They are just as courageous in illness, but the car, the radio and the television have brought more contact with the outside world.

# 9.

# The Churchman

From the Wordsworthian it is but a blurred footstep to the churchman. Many have tried to define Kilvert's churchmanship and the Rev. D.T.W. Price of St David's College, Lampeter has done it better than most. Perhaps before any systematic analysis of Kilvert's religious views be made, Wordsworth's observation could be quoted: "we murder to dissect". Kilvert never analysed his position within the wide range of opinion and practice of the Church of England and we must be well aware of the dangers of our judgements for religious climate and attitudes have changed very radically indeed.

He was brought up in a gentle mould both in schooltime and in holidays of Bible reading, family prayers and the reading aloud of sermons. So his religion was built into him. Whether he ever had a crisis of faith is extremely doubtful. Rebellion was not a part of his nature.

He never went to a theological college, like an ordinand in the Anglican Church of the last sixty-seventy years, so his theological framework was almost non-existent. But his faith in God was real indeed; it was tied and entwined in his poetic nature. That he was deeply read in the Bible and the Prayer Book is obvious for he often uses it for his own expression, not as a quotation but a part of his own speaking and writing.

What is debatable is whether he said the office of morning and evening service daily. He never says that he does and it is unlikely that he did. He said his prayers most regularly but often in thought form as he walked, especially in Langley beneath the trees of the Rectory garden.

Robert Kilvert, his father, was a good preacher but he seemed to be lax about the order of the service of Holy Communion in his church. His son belonged to a generation which was much more aware of the necessity of beauty and symbolism in worship. Yet he was not a high-churchman, he was far from impressed, by that position, and was a little sickened by Solemn Evensong at St. Barnabas' Church in Oxford. It was too long, the sermon was unoriginal and he did not like incense. In fact his sense of patriotism was affronted for he felt it was un-English and therefore disloyal. As one would expect he liked simplicity in religion, and he thought he saw it in the little Roman Catholic church nearby which appeared genuine and sincere because it was quiet and unflamboyant. In Dorset during Summer 1871 he attended Mass at the local church where a Mr Carn, late of the 14th Light Dragons, wore a green stole and "gabbled the prayers" and went "about the church to and fro, like a puppet on wires in a play. He was playing at Mass".

Kilvert, was, in fact, expressing what most Anglicans (a word not then in general parlance) felt. Today many find it difficult to understand the depth of feeling and emotion roused by the divisions amongst Christians. Ideas of the ecumenical movement were hardly conceived, let alone in infancy, and this was partly because of the Church of England's nature. It was a loosely defined institution, but based firmly in its doctine, working quite well but individually; each parish largely a little law to itself, and very dependent upon the incumbent who had no parochial church council to make known the feelings of the laity. The vicar worked with two wardens, one of his own choice and the other the people's elected at the Annual Parish Meeting, making all decisions.

Kilvert, brought up in this tradition, did not question it. But his faith in God and his knowledge of him was great, so he was not narrow minded. He was aware of other denominations and he had a romantic feeling towards the Catholics. Twice, to our knowledge, he went into the noble Roman Catholic Church in Bath where in 1875 "I knelt in the Church and prayed for charity, unity, and brotherly love, and the union of Christendom. Surely a Protestant may pray in a Catholic Church and be none the worse". Again in 1875 he spent a solemn half hour there.

At this time there was a resurgence of monasticism in this country both in the Roman Catholic and the Anglican Communion. Kilvert's chief contact with this phenomenon was through Father Ignatius Lyne, the eccentric deacon of the Church of England who established an ostensibly Benedictine monastery at Capel-y-Ffyn, close to Hay and still closer to the romantic and ever-haunting, some say haunted, Llanthony Abbey. The monastery at Capel-y-Ffyn was bought by Eric Gill in the 1920s and there along with the poet and painter David Jones he established a community of artists.

Kilvert walked over to see the monastery while it was under construction. He went there with his friend Morrell. Kilvert was curious and interested and clearly impressed that the masons regarded the monks with respect. Yet he, seeing them at work in the garden wearing their heavy habits, thought them like old women. He thought the healthy girl washing at the Chapel House was more natural and he uses the adjective 'morbid' to describe the life of the monks. One wonders whether Kilvert might have discovered more about Capel-y-Ffyn had he not been accompanied by the friendly but very worldly Morrell.

On the whole he did not like puritanical non-conformists. He saw in their churches much ugliness and often great lack of charity toward believers who strayed. But when a dissenting minister read the bible to one of his flock he was glad and not angered as had been anticipated.

At East Tytherton, close to Langley Burrell, there was a small community of Moravians. Their dignified small complex of fine eighteenth century houses, one the minister's house, one the chapel and the other the school, would appeal to the aesthetic sense. Then there was a family connection, for Kilvert's mother had been educated there, riding over from Langley Fitzurse rattling a bunch of keys in her donkey's ears to urge him on. They were more loyal too; they celebrated November 5th, burning Guy Fawkes' effigy! Perhaps he was kindly disposed because the Large family, well-known to his family, was kindly and generous: of Miss Large, Kilvert said she is "a true Good Samaritan". At this house Kilvert met Mr Wilson the minister and they talked happily and it seems to mutual benefit. Personal contact can overcome diverse barriers and with Kilvert this was particularly so.

Some have seen in Kilvert a purely social young man enjoying picnics and parties. That was a side of him, and the smaller side. In fact when one reads the unedited diaries one finds that William Plomer, even with all his tact, has shorn away a great deal of

Kilvert's parish work. He was an enthusiast; he loved preparing the young for Confirmation, and his piety rejoiced to see them presented to the bishop. He never grumbled at preparing yet another talk for the Communicant's Guild. He presided happily at a meeting in Langley after a busy day in London. And, more oddly to a clergyman of the 1980s, he never minded taking services and preaching when he was on holiday. Most present day clergy need a complete rest and even anonymity from their calling. The reason is not laziness or lack of faith; it is that the modern cleric is battling all the while against indifference or even concealed hostility. Kilvert was so fortunate, for he was swimming with a tide of faith. His task was much easier.

Recently Mrs Teresa Williams, an untiring Kilvert researcher, found in the *Hereford Times* of the 8th August 1868 a resumé of a sermon by Kilvert. This sermon tells us a great deal about the preacher and his vicar, Richard Lister Venables. It transpires that W.T.M. Baskerville of Clyro Court asked Kilvert to be his chaplain when he was High Sheriff for Radnorshire. This was a great honour for a young curate who was twenty eight at the time. There is no doubt that Kilvert immediately consulted his vicar about this and it speaks volumes for the generosity of Venables to his curate that he approved of the invitation. These small honours are jealously regarded and it shows not only Venables' magnanimity but also his maturity and sense of security. It was certainly a commendable gesture. It meant that Kilvert had to attend the Assizes in Presteigne with the High Sheriff and his retinue of javelin men at the opening of the commission, and Kilvert had to preach at the Assize Service in Presteigne Parish Church.

Often it has been wondered what Kilvert's sermons were like. We know his favourites, like the one called 'Mizpah', but none, it seemed, had survived. This one gives us a measure of his  preaching. His text was from the twelfth chapter of St Luke and the second verse: 'For there is nothing covered that shall not be revealed, neither hid that shall not be known'. A very suitable text for the occasion. He warns against the sin of the Pharisees, hypocrisy. A bold thing for a young man preaching to the bewigged establishment in all its might and power — and possibly having not a little self-righteousness. Very typically as we know him, he says

1. Claverton Lodge

2. Langley Burrell Rectory

3. Kilvert the schoolboy (third from left)

4. Francis Kilvert – Uncle

5. Adelaide Kilvert – Aunt

6. Robert Kilvert – Father

7. Thersie Smith – Sister

8. Revd. Richard Lister Venables

9. Mrs Agnes Venables

10. Dora Pitcairn – Sister

11. Edward Kilvert – Brother

12. Emily Wyndowe – Sister

13. The Wyndowe Children

14. Francis 'Daisy' Thomas

15. Ettie Meredith Brown

16. Katharine Heanley

17. Elizabeth Rowland

18. The Wedding of James and Dora Pitcairn

Back row from left: Mrs Thersie Smith (nee Kilvert); Mrs Laetitia Ashe; Miss Lucy Ashe; Revd. Robert Martin Ashe (The Squire); Miss Emily Ashe; Mr West Audrey; Mr James E Pitcairn, Bridegroom; Mrs Dora Pitcairn (nee Kilvert), Bride; Revd. Robert Kilvert, father; Mrs Thermuthis Kilvert, mother; Mr William Coleman; Mr Walter Coleman (?); Miss Elizabeth Rowland; Revd. Francis Kilvert; Miss Fanny Kilvert (?); Mrs Emily Wyndowe (nee Kilvert); Miss Thermuthis Ashe; Mr Edward Kilvert. Seated, foreground: Mr C D Pitcairn; Miss Florence Smith; Miss Pitcairn; the three Misses Wyndowe.

20. Francis Kilvert

19. Francis Kilvert and Elizabeth Rowland, enlarged from the wedding group

22. Bredwardine Vicarage

21. Clyro Church as painted by Thersie Smith

that God requires truth and that men shall love truth for its own sake of lovableness and beauty. That Kilvert should say 'lovableness' is apposite indeed. He then rather tritely points out that it is wiser to be true than false. God is a sleepless observer, but often gives no sign of his watchfulness. God's silence is interpreted by some as God's indifference.

Kilvert goes on to elaborate that a silent avenger dogs the footsteps of the criminal. The avenger rides with his victim, travelling in the guilty heart. He alludes to the fox beneath the cloak of the young Spartan who is eaten rather than reveal his secret. He then makes yet another classical allusion to Ibycus, an Athenian, who was murdered in the desert as cranes flew overhead. Some time later the robbers in a public place saw similar birds and one said: "Look the cranes of Ibycus" This was overheard and led to their arrest and condemnation. Kilvert goes on to Cain and Abel, the little known Achan and the more familiar Ananias and Sapphira. He reiterates that hypocrisy is never safe. Truth is impregnable because it is simple and needs no hiding. Falsehood needs continual concealment.

He ends with the argument that detection of a crime is a blessing for it may bring amelioration of character; and with the question what is shall profit a man if he gain the whole world but lose his soul?

It is the sermon of a young man who is packing in a lot of his knowledge for a learned congregation. It carries with it, though, conviction. I myself feel that Kilvert is as much moved by the classical stories as those of the Bible, which would be true of such a literary young man. Only at the end does it seem to falter. One feels he is in considerable sympathy with the offender, and he justifies rather than applauds the punishment. It is a very moral sermon, and it is precisely there that Kilvert the clergyman differs from his counterpart of today. The present-day clergyman is more alert and alive to theology and ideals but less, it would seem on the surface, to morality. Kilvert was of his age, and so a moral man. His most quoted and respected poem was called 'Honest Work'.

He wore his morality with humour though, and the present writer can here offer one autobiographical note. My boyhood was spent largely in Winchester, where I met many elderly retired clergy, and they were a benevolent, gentle, well-bred and well-read company. They talked ably of many things, and religion was entwined with Herbert, Shakespeare, Cowper. They had old-fashioned and well furnished minds but they raised amusement in me when they referred to Tennyson as 'a modern poet' in the late forties of this century. But in those old men I could see clearly the clan to which Kilvert belonged. They resembled R.S. Thomas's 'Country Clergy':

> I see them working in old rectories
> By the sun's light, by candlelight,
> Venerable men, their black cloth
> A little dusty, a little green
> With holy mildew. And yet their skulls,
> Ripening over so many prayers,
> Toppled into the same grave
> With oafs and yokels. They left no books,
> Memorial to their lonely thought
> In grey parishes; rather they wrote
> on men's hearts and in the minds
> Of young children sublime words
> Too soon forgotten. God in his time
> Or out of time will correct this.

Some of this applies to Kilvert, but he is exceptional in one clear sense. He did leave books.

It was Miss Bynon of Pentwyn in Clyro who really summed up Kilvert's faith. We can rely upon her judgement: she was an exceptional woman, as we have seen. When Kilvert returned to Clyro to take duty, some time after he had left she said to his face: "I was very happy to hear on Sunday that you had not lost your piety." It was this very piety, worn so easily, that made him so approachable and acceptable to many. His religion could be distilled into a quotation from the Epistle of St. James: "Pure religion and undefiled before God and the Father is this, to visit the fatherless and widows in their affliction, and to keep himself unspotted from the world." The visiting of the unfortunate, the desperately poor and the shunned was Kilvert's joy. It was, he considered, the major part of his ministry.

# 10.

# The Venables

When Kilvert became his curate in 1865, Richard Lister Venables had very recently lost his wife, Mary Augusta. So it was that Kilvert found a lonely man as his vicar, and from the short even terse diary of Venables we find that the curate often dined with the widower. They walked together and a very real relationship, somewhat paternal on Venables' part, sprang into being.

Richard Lister Venables was the product of a thriving earnest family who had had property since they followed the Conqueror from France to England. In the seventies Kilvert visited the small town of Venables, thirty miles from Rouen, and sought some memorials of the family, but without success. The Venables were small landowners who by shrewd marriages and hard work had continued to improve their place in society. The father of Richard Lister was another Richard who was a fellow of Clare College, Cambridge, and who on his marriage to Sophia Lister became vicar of Warmfield in Yorkshire. Then in 1811 he was nominated to the living of Clyro and became a Prebendary of Llansantffraed in the Collegiate Church of Christ College Brecon. This was the lovely area of the Usk with the castle of Tretower nearby where the twin brothers Henry and Thomas Vaughan were born on an April night in 1622. Both went to university, but it was Henry who returned to practise medicine and, in a small area, to write some of Britain's finest metaphysical verse.

Richard Lister was of a more practical habit of mind and, like his son Richard, a man of action on committees. In 1832 he was appointed Archdeacon of Carmarthen. He resigned Clyro to his son in 1847. He had lived at Llysdinam Hall, then a comparatively small country house, since 1830.

His three sons were Richard Lister, George Stovin and Joseph

Henry. Richard followed in his father's footsteps most precisely, becoming vicar of Clyro, Chairman of the Radnorshire Quarter Sessions and eventual owner of Llysdinam Hall. He was never made a Canon, or raised to any place in the hierarchy of the church. This could have been due to a coolness that existed between the Bishop of St David's and himself. Venables had little regard for the very learned bishop. It was a classic case of the dislike and suspicions engendered between the meeting of the man of action and the academic. The Bishop of St David's Connop Thirlwall, was always the scholar. This could also explain why Kilvert subsequently was slow to gain preferment.

George Stovin Venables became a barrister noted for his quick mind and his scorn for notes when in Court, but above all as a writer. He wrote for the *Saturday Review*, *The Spectator* and the *Foreign Quarterly Review*. Kilvert greatly enjoyed his company and his stories of literary London. Joseph Henry is a more shadowy figure.

After two years of widowerhood Richard Lister re-married. He chose for his bride Agnes Minna Pearson, one of the four daughters of Colonel Henry Shepherd Pearson of the Indian Civil Service. Colonel Pearson had served in the Crimean War as Aide-de-Camp to General Sir George Grigg. He told Kilvert the horrifying story that typifies so much of that much mismanaged and unnecessary war, how a French Officer arrived with a message about an attack. The General knew no French so he said to his Aide: "What does he say, Master Dick? Give him a glass of sherry and tell him to go away". As Kilvert said " '*Tell him to go away*!' As if he had been an organ-grinder! And', said Colonel Pearson with an expressive shrug, perhaps next morning a hundred lives might depend upon that message".

Agnes Minna was a plump little lady and in later years looked like a more genial version of Queen Victoria. Like the sovereign she had a determined desire for her own way, but she wielded this with charm and sympathy. She was, throughout her life, a receiver of others' pent up troubles. She was a good listener and sympathetic and discreet over Kilvert's outpourings of his love for Daisy Thomas.

But Agnes Minna had three other sisters, and two of them became friends of Kilvert. One married the Rev Sterling Browne

Westhorp, who became rector of Ilston on the Gower Peninsula and with whom Kilvert had two notable holidays. They were kind and hospitable.

Another sister married Captain Cowper Coles of the Royal Navy. He was not only a naval man but also a designer of ships. He was highly thought of, but tragedy overtook him when in a terrible storm in the Channel on 10th September 1870 his latest ship, a turret ship, overturned drowning five hundred men. It was said that when the ship was being built the shipbuilders altered the size of the freeboard causing the ship to capsize. It was, however, a terrible storm. The most august survivor was the Empress Eugenie fleeing from France in the yacht of Sir John Burgoyne. Another curious coincidence was that the ship had as its captain another Burgoyne, Hugh Burgoyne V.C. a close friend as well as relative of Sir John.

The Cowper Coles lived in a pleasant villa in Shanklin on the Isle of Wight. There Kilvert seemed very much part of the family and he spent more than one holiday with them, enjoying the sea, the young family and the island. He dug sandcastles and trenches and watched the happy children paddling. It was on the beach there that he experienced one of his passionate cravings for children. The cry turns one's heart nearly a hundred and fifteen years later.

> Oh, as I watched them there came over me such a longing, such a hungry yearning to have one of those children for my own. Oh that I too had a child to love and to love me, a daughter with such fair limbs and blue eyes archly dancing, and bright clustering curls blown wild and golden in the sunshine and sea air. It came over me like a storm and I turned away hungry at heart and half envying the parents as they sat upon the sand watching their children at play.

Indirectly we are indebted to Mrs Cowper Coles for this sharp insight into Kilvert. He longed, very naturally, for marriage, but he longed even more to be a father; and when later Mrs Cowper Coles realised that her son Sam needed coaching, she entrusted him to Kilvert's care and tuition.

A fourth sister, Augusta, he seems never to have met. Recently, her lively little diary called *A Spinster's Tour through North Wales in search of the Picturesque and Sentimental* has been published. It is enthusiastic, detailed and humorous. Had she met Kilvert one imagines there would have been natural recognition of so much common ground in temperament, expression and keen observation.

The three sisters were good friends, but none were so close, so concerned about Kilvert as Agnes Minna and her husband, and Agnes proved a friend and confidante beyond the grave. They all took to Kilvert and through them Kilvert was able to meet many interesting people. They widened the horizons of his life very considerably. When Kilvert met Venables it was a very fortunate encounter for him.

# 11.

# Aunt Maria

Virginia Woolf considered the description by Kilvert of his aunt's funeral to be the funniest in the English language. William Plomer wrote in his introduction to Volume I: "if [this account] were a chapter in a novel on the same level that novel would be a masterpiece."

This episode in Kilvert's life began on 29th November 1870 when he received a letter from his mother telling him of the death of Maria Kilvert of Worcester. Maria was a wealthy spinster, the daughter of Canon Richard Kilvert, who was a brother to Kilvert's grandfather. Richard Kilvert had been chaplain to Bishop Hurd of Worcester. He had been made a canon of the cathedral there and he had several livings besides. When he died he left a not inconsiderable fortune. His widow and daughter lived in Worcester and finally moved into 10 College Green, a house which is now the Deanery of Worcester.

Maria became increasingly eccentric, virtually a recluse, and bore a deep grudge against the Francis Kilvert of Bath who had written a bland and quite inoffensive biography of Bishop Hurd. Her own father had projected the work but had never achieved it. She thus resented that Francis had done it, most probably using material her father had provided. She lived alone, attended by her servants. As their mistress declined they became possessive and hostile to outsiders, as the Kilvert family were to discover. Miss Kilvert's main preoccupation was the restoration of the cathedral to which she made several generous gifts, £600 to the main fund and £300 to the work on the bells.

The Kilverts wondered, quite naturally, whether they might inherit something from her. When Robert Kilvert and his wife journeyed up to Worcester at the wish of the solicitor, they thought that the bulk of her fortune would go to the cathedral. Kilvert received a letter from his mother in Worcester complaining of the attitude of the servants, who at first told them that there was no bed for them in the house and no food. So they stayed in an hotel until the solicitor, next day, said that they had every right to lodge in the house. Even so the servants hired a charwoman to wait upon the Kilverts, their resentment was so great.

The Will had been revealed to the parents. The sum of £15000 was left to charities, Clergy Widows and Orphans and Home Missions and the Society for the Propagation of the Gospel. The diarist called this "a piece of ostentation and a most erroneous injustice." The sum of £600 had been left to Lord Lyttleton but had been revoked. There is no evidence that the old lady even knew him. The fine prints she left to the Bishop of Worcester. When all debts and expenses had been paid the residue was to be divided between his father, Aunt Marianne and the Motherwells. "A most iniquitous will, not a shilling was left to any of the Francis Kilverts, the old grudge and malice against Uncle Francis for writing Bishop Hurd's life ruling strong in death".

Kilvert went to Worcester on the train, meeting by chance a lady who had lived in Warsaw. She talked of Poland and Russia, she interested him and she gave him some very garbled information about the Russian Royal Family. In Worcester he made for College Green and his parents. What then follows for several pages is perfect and completely detached reportage written with the quiet irony which Kilvert so often used. He was announced by the maid as "A visitor for Mrs Kilvert" and as he entered saw his mother removing her spectacles (a very Victorian gesture) to receive a stranger.

Food was brought on a tray by a charwoman, for the servants, no doubt anticipating wealth in Miss Kilvert's will, were far too proud to wait upon the unwelcome relatives. Without any emotion Kilvert was led to see the dead lady:

> The coffin lid with its brass breastplate leaned upright in a corner of the room. The face that lay still, frozen down into silence, in the coffin was a very remarkable one. It was a distinguished face with aristocratic features. A firm mouth, fine highly formed nose delicately and sharply cut. There was a slight frown and a contraction of the brows. It was the face of a person of

considerable ability, stern, severe, and perhaps a little contemptuous, an expression which with the contraction of the brows was so habitual that death had smoothed neither away.

Although he saw "a likeness to some one of the race" and a strong resemblance to his father, he was not drawn to her at all. He liked better the proof prints which hung in the drawing room: "the most exquisite engravings I ever saw, so soft and clear". Kilvert always chooses the right adjective: these pictures now in Clyro Church may not appeal to late twentieth century taste but they are soft and clear.

The funeral next day found Kilvert and his father the chief mourners, but Kilvert saw the entire proceedings with sardonic dispassion:

The bearers had been selected not at all with reference to their fitness for the task, but with reference to the friendship entertained for them by the servants of the house. One of the bearers on the right side was very short, so short that he could not properly support the coffin level. The coffin seemed very heavy. As the procession moved across College Green to the Cloister arch, the men staggered under the weight and the coffin lurched and tilted to one side over the short bearer. One very fat man had constituted himself chiefest mourner of all and walked next to the coffin before my Father and myself. The bearers, blinded by the sweeping pall, could not see where they were going and nearly missed the Cloister arch, but at length we got safe into the narrow dark passage and into the Cloisters. The great bell boomed high overhead and the deep thrilling vibrations hung trembling in the air long after the stroke of the bell.

So the clergy and choir came to meet us at the door, then turned and moved up the Cathedral nave chanting in solemn procession, 'I am the Resurrection and the Life saith the Lord'. But meanwhile there was a dreadful struggle at the steps leading up from the Cloisters to the door. The bearers were quite unequal to the task and the coffin seemed crushingly heavy. There was a stamping and a scuffling, a mass of struggling men swaying to and fro, pushing and writhing and wrestling while the coffin sank and rose and sank again. Once or twice I thought the whole mass of men must have been down together with the coffin atop of them and some one killed or maimed at least. But now came the time of the fat chief mourner. Seizing his opportunity he rushed into the strife by an opening large and the rescued coffin rose. At last by a wild effort and tremendous heave the ponderous coffin was borne up the steps and through the door into the Cathedral where the choristers, quite unconscious of the scene and the fearful struggle going on behind, were singing up the nave like a company of angels. In the Choir there was another dreadful struggle to let the coffin down. The bearers were completely overweighted, they bowed and bent nearly fell and threw the coffin down on the floor.

The tragi-comedy was not over. The Will was read. "The estate proved to be £36000 and about £7000 will come to my Father. When he left Langley he did not even know if he should have enough left him to pay his expenses. The cook was entirely ignored, except £5 for mourning like the others. The other two servants had £100 apiece. Charlotte, the ladies' maid, asked Mr Hooper to announce this fact to the cook himself. She was summoned and he broke the news to her. She retired in dudgeon and I expect the other servants had a breezy time of it as the cook was said to be a bad-tempered woman."

All Kilvert got was a seal worth half-a-crown which he had no compunction in pocketing as expenses for his support at the occasion. Possibly the legacy to his father was lessened to £5000, but it was still a very agreeable amount in those days.

Here we pause and wonder what would have happened if Robert Kilvert had inherited considerably more. It would have enabled him to retire with his wife and two unmarried daughters. By arrangement the living of Langley could have been conveyed to his son. Had that happened the course of Kilvert's story might have been very different. He might have married Daisy, and then there would have been neither Ettie Meredith Brown nor Katherine Heanley in his life, and Elizabeth Rowland might never have been heard of at all. Whether Kilvert would have been any happier in Langley as incumbent is debatable. The old suspicions between the great house and the rectory would have rumbled on causing misery and dissatisfaction to both houses. It is a surmise of ifs and buts and perhapses.

# 12.

# Love

No thorns go as deep as a rose's
And love is more cruel than lust
Swinburne

In September 1871 Kilvert was in a ferment of feeling. He had fallen in love. He was thirty years old, he had a normal sexual temperature and was entirely heterosexual. Before this love there must have been other attractions but we know nothing of them. By his beliefs, his upbringing and very much because of his place as a priest in society he was denied outlets to his normal sexuality. George Bernard Shaw would have considered him a victim of middle-class morality. Had he been born into faster and more aristocratic circles, or into the farming community by which he was surrounded, his repression would have been much the less.

He adored pretty faces and he saw many. His particular penchant in his loneliness was for the beauty of little girls. In summer 1870 he was quite infatuated by Elizabeth Jones, whom he called Gipsy Lizzie. His descriptions of her at that time are surprising to us even a hundred years later.

> Gipsy Lizzie has been put into my reading class. How is the indescribable beauty of that most lovely face to be described — the dark soft curls parting back from the pure white transparent brow, the exquisite little mouth and pearly tiny teeth, the pure straight delicate features, the long dark fringes and white eyelids that droop over and curtain her eyes, when they are cast down or bent upon her book . . . Oh, child, child, if you did but know your own power. Oh, Gipsy, if only you grow up as good as you are fair.

There is something of eroticism there. He is dramatising his

83

feelings, but the unconscious censor of his mind makes him use the word pure, it is used twice and then turns all his emotion into a benediction.

A paragraph later he mentions Clavering Lyne, an extremely extrovert young man and brother of the Father Ignatius who was building the monastery at Capel-y-Ffyn. Lyne aroused Kilvert's ire for he pursued and teased Fanny Thomas of Llanigon at croquet, and Kilvert was jealous. This is the first mention of Fanny, whom he always called Daisy.

At this time his amorous temperature was high and on a Monday morning he looks up at the farm of Penllan and goes into a rhapsody. It is pure pre-Raphaelite, and with a clear echo of Keats' 'The Eve of St. Agnes'.

> The sweet grey eyes that have long been open and looking upon the pearly morning sky and the mists of the valley and the morning spread upon the mountains, and think of the young busy hands that have long been at work, milking or churning, with the sleeves rolled up the round arms as white and creamy as the milk itself, and the bright sweet morning face that the sunrise and the fresh early air have kissed into bloom and the sunny tresses ruffled by the mountain wind, and hope that the fatherless girl may ever be good, brave, pure and true. So help her God. The sun looks through her window which the great pear tree frames and lattices in green leaves and fruit, and the leaves move and flicker and throw a chequering shadow upon the white bedroom wall, and on the white curtains of the bed. And before the sun has touched the sleeping village in the shade below or has even struck the weathercock into a golden gleam, or has crept down the steep green slope of the lower or upper Bron, he has stolen into her bedroom and crept along the wall from chair to chair till he has reached the bed, and has kissed the fair hand and arms that lies upon the coverlet and the white bosom that heaves half uncovered after the restlessness of the sultry night, and has kissed her mouth whose scarlet lips, just parting in a smile and pouting like rosebuds to be kissed, show the pearly gleam of the white teeth, and has kissed the sweet face and the blue veined silky lashed eye-lids and the white brow and the soft bright tangled hair, till she has unclosed the sweetest eyes that ever opened to the dawn, and risen and unfastened the casement and stood awhile breathing the fresh fragrant

mountain air as it blows . . .

This self-indulgent writing then veers towards safety. It speaks in the same tones of prayer, drawing water at St Mary's well and going about "honest, holy work, all day long, with a light heart and a pure conscience."

This is the writing of an overcharged man, in love with love. He is Shakespeare's Duke Orsino. It is a clear signal of his emotional state, for he is more than ready for love; he is ready for bed. It seems for a moment he will fall in love not with Gipsy, not with Daisy Thomas, but Miss Lyne, with her "beautiful little hand just what a lady's hand ought to be, small, soft, white, warm and dry". But, no, she leaves Hay with her brother and his four dogs.

Kilvert then goes on holiday in July 1870. One feels a change of the highly charged air will be salutary. His destination is Cornwall where he stays with friends who had lived briefly in Langley Burrell; they were William and Emma Hockin: their home Tullimaar was one they had inherited and moved to in 1869. The notebook of this holiday very wondrously escaped all severe and emasculating censorship. Recently it has been published with the benefit of sensitive and thorough scholarship. Kilvert was drawn to Emma Hockin. They shared many interests; Tennyson, a love of romantic scenery, and ferns and flowers. Their temperaments seemed in tune and Kilvert, so intensely alive to the sights and sounds of Celtic Cornwall around him, was unusually receptive and perceptive. He was, as he said more than once, in a dream. It was a dream a little irritated at times by the heartiness of William Hockin. Richard Maber (editor of the original version of the Cornish Section) has recognised a quotation there which reveals much:

> Sunday 24th July
> The privacy, quietness and deep peacefulness of this place is very delightful particularly on Sundays. In the afternoon we had coffee out in the summer house and sat there talking till the heat of the day had abated. Aside the devil turned etc. etc. Ah, how intelligible.

The quotation is from Milton's *Paradise Lost*, Book IV lines 502-

511 and reads:

> . . . . aside the devil turned
> For envy, yet with jealous leer malign
> Eyed them askance, and to himself thus plained:
> Sight hateful, sight tormenting! Thus these two,
> Imparadis'd in one another's arms,
> The happier Eden, shall enjoy their fill
> Of bliss, on bliss, while I to hell am thrust,
> Where neither joy nor love, but fierce desire,
> Among our other torments not the least,
> Still unfulfilled with pain of longing pines.

Unconsciously by some movement, glance or touch of hands, the married couple had aroused such longings for a similar married state in the warm blooded curate. One feels for him. One is also thankful that his Uncle Francis at his school in Claverton Lodge had so taught his nephew that in a small crisis of this kind he was able to identify himself with literature and so to some extent sublimate his passion.

He returned to Clyro in an extremely busy year socially, and in the parish the fever abated. His longing to give and receive affection was channelled into such tasks as helping Dr Clouston of Hay hold Annie Corfield whilst he put back her dislocated elbow. His compassion is aroused and at the same time frustrated for the motherless children who were flogged mercilessly by their father.

It was in September that Kilvert went to the large house Llanthomas in the parish of Llanigon. It is a small village four miles from Hay and closer to the Black Mountains. William James Thomas, formerly Vicar of Gladestry, exchanged livings with the incumbent of Llanigon; he bought Llanthomas and lived there with his large family for the remainder of his life. He was a man of means, a squarson, and had six sons and five daughters.

When Kilvert went to play croquet there, Frances Eleanor Jane was aged eighteen and had just left school. She felt grown up and as independent as a young Victorian lady could feel. Against her father's wishes she sat by Kilvert during supper. One suspects that her father was alert to the attractions of the handsome young clergyman. He was to prove a vigilant father and possibly a jealous one.

During supper Kilvert told her of a sick child, Alice Davies of

Cwm Sir Hugh, who was in his class:

> She became interested and when she heard what a treat fruit
> was to the sick child she sent the footman for a dish of grapes.
> 'Here' she said, taking two bunches and putting them on my
> plate, 'take her these'. 'I do like you for that' I said earnestly, 'I
> do indeed'. She laughed. I think she was pleased. I demurred
> about taking them. So when the ladies rose she went coaxingly
> up to her father and to satisfy me asked if she might send the
> grapes to the sick child. 'Certainly' he said. So she said she
> would put the grapes in a little basket and be sure to give them
> to me when I went away. Today I fell in love with Fanny
> Thomas'.

This was Friday 8th September 1871. All the usual symptoms of
love were now experienced; restlessness, day-dreaming,
sleeplessness. He unburdened himself to Mrs Venables without,
at first, divulging the name of his beloved. She relayed the news
to her much occupied husband who took a more brusque and
matter-of-fact attitude to the whole affair and dismissed the
matter for another day. So another day of feverish insecurity,
hopes and anticipations and a terrible fear of loss ensued. After
talking with Mrs Venables on the lawn, Kilvert went off to
propose, or at least sound out Mr Thomas.

It was again in the garden, within earshot of the gardener, that
Kilvert made his avowal of love for Daisy. The poor young man
was embarrassed when he thought he had been overheard, but
Mr Thomas assured him that the gardener was deaf. He was,
alas, as deaf as Mr Thomas was to Kilvert's intentions. As we
learn later, Mr Thomas said to his wife, "That little Fanny likes
Mr Kilvert." The father was sensitive and alert, but adamant
against the pursuit of the courtship. Like many high-minded
Victorians who preached on 'eyes of needles and rich men
entering Paradise', considering them no doubt comforting to the
poor, in practice he sided with hard headed business acumen. It
was all disguised beneath discussion of her youth, and the horrors
of long engagements. He enjoined Kilvert "not [to] show her that
you like her more than the others. It is a cruel thing for you, I
know, but it would be a still more cruel thing to tell her and
destroy her peace of mind".

As so often with older men Kilvert allowed himself to be over-
ruled. He had a fatal tendency to submit to authority. He was also
well nigh penniless and his prospects were not encouraging.
Money, something he rarely alludes to, is borne in upon him as a
vital factor in life. It is a bitter blow to him, and because he is so
open and honest in his diary, readers who are older and more
securely placed in life tend to regard it all with a smiling
indulgence. Audiences laugh, and his entries invite it: "Lying in
bed this morning dozing, half awake and half asleep, I composed
my speech of thanks at my wedding breakfast, a very affecting
speech." He still harbours hopes but does nothing to buttress
them.

On a Sunday at this time his much loved sister Dora
accompanied him on the long walk to Bettws. He must have
dragged his feet, for in his heart was heavy and he says that his
sister "skipped about like a goat". Though quite evidently his
favourite sister he does not seem to have confided in her. That
same Sunday he had received a letter from his father which
harked back to his disappointment at the will of Maria Kilvert.
Had her will shown more sense of family affection he might have
retired from Langley in his son's favour. As it is, they cannot
afford that luxury. He tells his son that one day he will inherit
£2700. This was a not inconsiderable sum but hardly a
competency. Kilvert's means were summed up in the phrase
'genteel poverty'.

What one wonders were Daisy's thoughts? There is no doubt
that she was in love. In a small society they were bound to meet.
Kilvert notes her wearing "black velvet jacket and light dress,
with a white feather in her hat and her bright golden hair tied up
with blue riband. How bright and fresh and happy and pretty she
looked."

A little later, 20th September he sees her at Hay Castle where
she appeared: "more quiet, guarded and reserved . . . it seemed
to me as if she had received a hint not to be too forthcoming".
Three days later he received a letter from Mr Thomas which he
describes as cordial, but which gave Kilvert no hope whatsoever
and told him to put away all thoughts of Daisy.

In November he sees her at Hay Castle where the combined
Beavan and Thomas families had been marched and drilled by

Captain John Thomas. The idle had to find occupations to fill the empty hours. What is even more revealing is that Fanny Beavan had to return to school, and no doubt she was bemoaning this fact. fact. Daisy burst out: "I wish that I had lessons to do". As time was to prove, Daisy had a lively mind interested in many things and was full of energy. A photograph of her not long before her death in 1928 shows not the round face and slightly podgy girl, but a fine featured face, aristocratic and vivacious.

Both Kilvert and Daisy were victims of an unjust economic system and an unthinking acceptance of a social code, and both were sacrificed to its inexorable demands. One wonders whether, if they had been in England or closer to London or some other progressive city, this code would have prevailed. For in many places it was already eroding, and girls were finding their freedom. The Thomases, like other families who seemed so grand in the Border country, would not have appeared so splendid in the Home Counties; they would have seemed no more than upper middle class. Isolation in the country fosters *folie de grandeur* still.

This same day Kilvert finds that he has come away from Llanthomas with the wrong walking stick, and he says to Daisy that he will return it. The girl so suddenly becoming a woman blurts out: "Yes — and come *very soon*". This made hope flare again in Kilvert's imagination and he writes: "I wonder if Daisy and I will ever read these pages over together. I think we shall". Many times at bazaars and church gatherings he encountered her. "she seemed shy and reserved and I thought troubled, and I fancied she avoided me". At Llanthomas once more he envies Sailor, the black retriever, which was pressed against her side.

There is a rueful note that Daisy 'came out' at the Hereford Hunt Ball and that she had been very much admired. With even more alarm he hears that the officers from Brecon had been invited by Mr and Mrs Thomas to a dinner party. It was Mrs Bevan who kindly and perceptively said to him that they were all married men.

The parents could not keep their daughter in seclusion, for that would defeat their plans for a 'good' marriage. Neither could they ensure that Kilvert would not be of the company. The couple met again at a Clifford Priory dance in April, they sat out behind an azalea and Mr Thomas broke in upon them and demanded Daisy's attendance at the next dance. This was a polite war, but war nonetheless. The dance revived all Kilvert's feelings, and no doubt Daisy's too. He wrote that "I can rest nowhere in my misery".

Two years later, in March 1874, he is at Three Cocks Railway Station and he sees a tall girl in deep mourning. It is Daisy. In a low voice she said: "I have been looking out for you for such a long time". Kilvert saw her sad sweet face, he detected reproach and helplessly that day he wrote: "Poor child, my poor child". Then after another parting, "I saw the anguish of her soul. What could I do?"

What could he do? He accepted authority, and he had promised her father not to speak of his love, so the poor girl was left bewildered. I feel there is no doubt she loved him. I do not doubt his love for her, but he did not treat her well. This was much deeper than his other sudden obsessions with young women like Mary Bevan, Marion Vaughan and Florence Hill. This was not Kilvert's last love affair, possibly not even his unhappiest, as will be seen later, but it cannot be dismissed. Some have called it naive. That adjective can be applied to all true romantic love, for without it the love can be calculating and not true love.

This love was mutual and it was simple. It is true that eleven years divided them in age, but Kilvert was not an early developer and Daisy was conscious of his desire for her. He was not foolish to imagine her by his side in a vicarage. It would have been a role she would have enjoyed and fulfilled excellently.

The key words of this episode are "What could I do?" He could have broached the matter with Mr Thomas again. He could have seen the Bishop and discussed prospects for a living of his own. He could have enlisted the support of his vicar and friend, Mr Venables. But, apparently, almost certainly he did none of these things. This lays bare a curious facet of Kilvert's character; he was, in spite of his emotions, a passive man. He allowed events, circumstances, and the pressures of his time to mould his life. He was in the truest sense a non-combatant. He accepted too mildly the rigorous conventions which in spite of insistence on breeding and education, were based very soundly upon money as well. The first two he could claim, but he allowed lack of the third to cripple him.

He could have sought a better paid curacy, but he was inhibited, a word that often springs to mind when writing of him, but even more frequently of this time. His family loyalty impeded him. He had agreed tacitly with his father that a seven year curacy in Clyro, like Laban's in the Old Testament, should be served before he returned to Langley.

More than a century later, "an empire and two wars away", we can see the tyranny that family life could wield, and how it spread through the hierarchical structure of society. In the Thomas family it is obviously apparent, but Kilvert senior, for all his kindliness, is not untainted either. He loved his elder son dearly, but did not see that he had a need to lead a life of his own, to make a career as his younger son was doing in the Civil Service. But the younger son, Edward (often called 'Perch') was almost of another generation. Unlike his brother he was not educated in such private circumstances by an uncle. He went to Marlborough, so Edward belonged to another wave of the middle classes adhering to a new scheme which in its turn became more rigid and hidebound. Francis was among the last of the early Victorians; his education links him with *David Copperfield*. Edward belongs to the world of *Tom Brown's Schooldays*.

There are times when Francis comes very close to being like the subject of a novel by George Gissing; one of the genteel poor, the governesses, the intellectually able who were economically underprivileged.

Daisy Thomas and her sisters never escaped either. None of the girls were to marry. Daisy was to remain at Llanthomas all her life, filling it with good works in the parish and various arts and crafts. The present writer knew an elderly clergyman who had been one of 'her boys' in a class she ran. He remembered her with amusement and affection. He remembered, too, a youthful embarrassment. She taught him to swim in the river Wye, and he loved the lessons and her company, but her serge bathing costume of antique design made him squirm. He feared the ridicule of his friends.

# 13.

# Summer 1870

In May 1870 Kilvert returned home to Langley to see his sister, Emily and her husband, Samuel Wyndowe, who were on leave from India. Sam was a Surgeon-General in the Indian Army. He was as a doctor humane and his sympathies strayed far beyond the confines of the barracks. He was appalled by the poverty of the native population and particularly distressed by the child-brides, many of whom died in childbirth at the age of twelve and thirteen. His desire was to help them, but the strict enforcement of purdah denied him any access to them. He was also a resourceful man, he set up the first medical school in Madras state for the training of Indian students. Another of his enterprises was to start a factory where shark oil could be refined, which could be used as a substitute for cod liver oil, to help combat malnutrition and hence tuberculosis.

Perhaps the strangest episode in his life was during the Mutiny, when he joined a troop of volounteer cavalry. Some mutineers were marching towards his hospital, he rallied his little troop, deserted his post at the hospital, led the charge and dispersed the enemy. For this action he received two letters, one of congratulation for his commendable valour and another condemning him for abandoning his hospital. This reminds one of Tolstoy who, during the Crimean War, was awarded a medal and reduced to the ranks at the same time.

The Wyndowes installed themselves with their children and their ayah, an elderly Indian woman. When Kilvert arrived Emily came running down the stairs to greet him. He met the children, he looked searchingly at Katie and minutely described her face, but when, Annie, the baby was brought to him wearing a long grey dress and practically bald, he immediately nick-named her 'The Monk'. He was captivated by this babe and bewilderingly refers to the tiny child as either him, or her.

He wheeled her about the garden in the 'chota gharry', a perambulator. He propelled her so swiftly that once he upset the entire contraption and the Monk howled vigorously at this rough treatment. When Edward, Kilvert's younger brother joined them, the two young men harnessed the dog to the 'chota gharry' and with the older child as passenger, with Kilvert leading the dog on the rope and Edward steering the carriage they ran up and down the lawn.

When Emily and Sam went back to India they left their children behind, the Empire was built on heartbreaks of this kind. The result was that Kilvert saw more of his nieces and there was a bond between 'The Monk' and him. Anne Mallinson, who knew 'The Monk' well, when a much older and widowed lady, suggests that there was a link in character between them, both were gentle, both had great depth of feeling and both had the strange power of attraction. Both were natural leaders in the small community of village life. She died in Gloucestershire on Easter-Day 1954.

Kilvert's affinity with children, almost an idealization of them, was something of his age, the innocence of childhood was lauded by many poets, including Wordsworth. Kilvert's fondness is a recurrent theme all through the diary and some children move him to rapture. A notable example was when he was travelling in a railway carriage in April 1874. He was allowed to nurse a small girl of three and his ecstasy was supreme:

> From the moment the child was in my arms a sudden and great happiness came over me. I had thought my heart was growing hard and that I was no longer capable of such emotion. But in an instant the old delicious feeling swept over me again, and once more there was only one thing in the world and that was love. I knew a man. Such as one caught up to the third heaven, and saw and felt unspeakable things. That has come true from the beginning of the world and will be true to its end, and as long as human nature shall last.

It is of interest that he so swiftly and naturally quotes St. Paul with a sense of identity in 1873. In 1870 there was a note of the erotic in his lyricism when he describes the sun creeping round the room at early morn in Penllan, but that was the passionate and febrile summer of 1870 to which we must return.

On Tuesday 21st June 1870, whilst his father and brother Edward were staying with him, there took place one of the great picnics of English literature. A whole party of local people had decided to drive to Snodhill Castle. There was a procession of four carriages and other horses, "girls ran out into the porches of the quaint picturesque old fashioned farm houses of the Golden Valley to see the string of horses and carriages, and the gay dresses of the ladies".

The way is still pretty, and when the main road from Dorstone is left it becomes quiet and begins to achieve that special remoteness of parts of Herefordshire. They passed the Court Farm, a fine stone house, probably Jacobean, and built from the stone of the castle. The mount Kilvert describes as steep and slippery. It still is, but the view westwards is an English idyll; fields, farms, little woods and hills, — the sight almost brings Vaughan Williams music to the inner ear.

Here the young men and women lit a fire to boil potatoes in a pot. They spilt it, the tripod of sticks burnt and everyong gave conflicting advice. They did not go hungry, the humble potatoes were rescued and "there was plenty of meat and drink, the usual things, cold chicken, ham and tongue, pies of different sorts, salads, jam and gooseberry tarts, bread and cheese. Splendid strawberries from Clifford Priory brought by the Haigh Allens. Cup of various kinds went round, claret and hock, champagne, cider and sherry, and people sprawled about in all attitudes and made a great noise."

They went back to Dorstone Rectory where after dinner the carpet in the drawing room was rolled up and they danced. Rather typically in spite of the gusto with which the day's activities have been described, he adds "The drive home in the cool of the evening was almost the pleasantest part of the day".

Robert Kilvert and his son Edward fished at Llangorse. Edward was a keen naturalist and, though Kilvert could outwalk his younger brother, it is Edward who sees the animals and birds. When out with his brother Kilvert sees much much more than when alone. As one reads the few surviving unedited notebooks one begins to think that Kilvert is unnecessarily tiring his brother who sleeps in the grass whilst the curate visits a farm. A little later one learns that Edward is ill in London, and obviously had not been feeling strong at the time. Whereas Kilvert abounds in energy.

The three men are in wonderful accord and Kilvert senior, looking at Clyro "expressed his admiration of the scene. He said he used to think Keevil beautiful in its way, but that it was not to be compared to Clyro for loveliness". The old man appreciates his son's love for the place with a total understanding and he is very tactful. It is only as they walk together to the station that he raises the subject of his son's possible return to Langley: "We made the Seven Years Convention about Clyro and Langley". This section of the diary was omitted by William Plomer, yet from it we see quite clearly that Kilvert intended to leave Clyro in 1872. He was adhering to the old biblical tradition of the seven years' service.

However, a little more was to happen before that. There is the holiday in Cornwall and the mutual love with Daisy Thomas, as we have seen, and the funeral of Maria Kilvert. There is also the famous skating day at Draycot (near Chippenham) in December 1870.

But it is also now his mother's turn to come and stay. She neither walks nor fishes, so Kilvert is not with her as much. Two days before she left to return home, they went to the Crichtons and Wye Cliff, where were "one of the prettiest archery grounds I ever saw, the high woods above and the river below". It is still called the Archery Field and still has its woods and the winding Wye. The occasion moved him to write very lyrically and very tellingly: "It was a pretty sight to see the group of ladies with their fresh light dresses moving up and down the long green meadow between the targets, and the arrows flitting and glancing white to and fro against the bank of dark green trees". I can never read that without a mental image of Monet's 'Femmes au Jardin' springing to my mind, the dresses billowing and those arrows, flitting, glancing. It is impressionism in words.

Kilvert liked society but it was, that summer, meeting too frequently and there seems a sigh and weariness when he describes the friends as "the usual set that one meets and knows so well". He thought of learning archery to shoot instead of merely score, for he was a little bored. But it went deeper than this, and a portion of him was unfulfilled. These people were good as companions, they shared a similar background, but he was in modern parlance 'his own man'. He did not share all their enthusiasms but he was much more alive to beauty than they. He was also, in a way, less inhibited. One wonders what the Beavans and Colonel Balmayne would have said had they known that the very acceptable young curate had written of Gypsy Lizzie so erotically, or even decorated his mantlepiece at Ashbrook with trails of hop bine. They would not have approved the first and the second would have been deemed unmanly. His family, however, accepted at least the second. The first they never knew about.

It was the artist in Kilvert rejoicing in all the manifold beauties of the day, trying to lengthen the joy by bringing the flowers to his room and better still recording the fascinating ephemera of the moment. It was a small stage. On the grander stage of Europe, Bismarck was watching the fading popularity of the Emperor Napoleon III and his wife, the Empress Eugenie. He awaited his time, and in 1870 suddenly France was at war with Prussia. Kilvert like most British people began by supporting the Prussians, but as France was crushed, especially at the battle of Sedan, opinion changed. The Emperor was pitied and the Empress's courage admired. The Franco-Prussian War was, in many ways, the foundation for the First World War which was to remove Kilvert's world from us so decisively.

But two years later, Kilvert's own immediate world underwent change too. For on 26th March 1872 he wrote a letter to the Bishop of St. David's giving his intention of resigning the curacy of Clyro. He added, on Mr Venables advice and against his own judgement, that he had been licensed in the diocese for seven and a half years. There is evidence that Kilvert, like most young curates, brought enthusiasm and vigour to the parish. Venables had discovered that he could leave things safely in his curate's hands whilst he was away in London or Llysdinam. He had appreciated this and raised Kilvert's salary at various times. There were gifts and presents of money every now and then. It had been a happy partnership.

In the parish there was talk of Kilvert taking over when the Venables family left — in fact Venables kept the living for another two years. This talk is the kind of gossip and idle speculation that parishes to this day indulge in. Very rarely indeed does a curate become vicar of the parish in which he serves, unless the church has a change of status and beomes a parish rather than the daughter church in a larger parish.

However, Mr Venables, probably seeing that the extensions to Llysdinam were slow and the house unfit for his young family, asked Kilvert to stay on and as an incentive offered him £160 a year, more, one suspects, than his father could afford to pay him. Kilvert remained firm to his decision. Possibly his unhappy love affair with Daisy helped him in his resolve. It upset him to see her and for her sake he thought it better that he was out of sight.

People were sorry to lose a friend and presents, many very handsome, rolled in for the departing curate including a gold watch from the Venables. His favourite present was a gold pencil case to hang from his watch chain given by the children of the school. They had saved the money over a long period, and many had stayed away from the fairs in order to preserve their little hoards for Mr Kilvert.

When the official farewell took place in the school Mr Wall, the churchwarden, presented Kilvert with a magnificent silver cup. The Butler of Clyro Court presented an ink stand from the staff and estate workers. Kilvert was so touched that he said very little in thanks. His emotion can be appreciated. His feelings certainly overcame him at his last service at Bettws chapel where he also preached. He took his text from St. Paul's epistle to the Philippians; 'The Prisoner of the Lord', "I thank my God upon every remembrance of you". During this he burst into tears. The new curate his successor, who had accompanied him, must have watched the spectacle with some surprise, thinking either that his predecessor was rather foolish, or that he would be a forerunner very hard to emulate.

On his last day he recalled his first day there: "I remember fixing my eyes on a particular bough of an apple tree in the orchard opposite the school and the Vicarage and saying to myself that on the day I left Clyro I would look at that same branch. I did look for it this morning but I could not recognise it".

He returned for a visit in March 1873. The old spell fell over him again, the views of the mountains, the children and the old folk. He found changes as well, more trees had gone, little Lily Crichton aged seven had died. So, too, had Edward Evans — dead, one hopes, before the cat ate him, for Kilvert had written: "Visited Edward Evans in the dark hole in the hovel roof which does duty for a bedroom, and a gaunt black and white ghostly cat was stalking about looking as if she were only waiting for the sick man to die, that she might begin on him".

He went up to Wernnewydd and Mrs Lloyd exclaimed with surprise when she saw him: "We sat and talked round the fire and the great yellow sheepdog old Mint came in like a lion barking furiously at seeing a stranger as he thought but then in a moment came and laid his head lovingly on my knee". This is the immemorial life of the farms, dogs, cats, animals, fires, working as long as light permits. It still continues, and I myself have had tea on a hill farm, a dog at my feet, listening to the sprightly chatter of the farmer's widow. Behind me at a great table, the farming son and a labourer were engaged in their own tea and their own talk. But there is a difference, for this lady showed me photographs of her daughter in Australia married to a Greek scientist with a great string of degrees. We talked of a chuch that Kilvert never mentions, the Greek Orthodox. Kilvert's world still exists, but it is no longer so confined.

# 14.

# Back to the Nest

The last entry on Clyro in 1872 quoted *Lycidas*: "To-morrow to fresh woods and pastures new". It was not at all accurate, for he went home, back to Langley Burrell Rectory. And when he opened his window next morning, 3rd September 1872: "the first sound I heard was the tapping of a nuthatch in an acacia".

There is a tendency to think that the Border Country meant everything to Kilvert. It most definitely evoked a response hardly equalled in his descriptions of anywhere else. Temperamentally, it suited him well. Often because of his love of it and its people he imagined he must have Welsh blood. It was the drama of the mountains, the closeness of the valleys, the shadows of the trees and the close knit families and their feuds that attracted him. One wishes that a projected walk to Glamorgan and the industrial area of South Wales had been achieved, for then he would have seen a very different Wales — slag heaps, mean housing, a great absence of any aesthetic quality in architecture.... What would his impressions have been? He would perhaps have rejoiced that so small a land could provide so many faces — each different, each with a differing landscape wrought by the subtle shift in inclines, plains and mountains.

To be home in Langley was initially no hardship, and Kilvert's delight in being a part of the family once more was very great. He was a creature of domestic inclination. His intense longing to be a father was a part of that adoration of the ideal of the family. The times that he was lonely in the two rooms at Ty Dulas in Clyro must have been many; they gave to posterity a wonderful journal, but we should not accept them without some acknowledgement of a certain lack of fulfilment. At home there were his sisters and parents to talk to of the things that before he only discussed and described on the empty page. The habit of recording however was there and it was to last.

No sooner had he unpacked his belongings, the accumulations of the Welsh years, than he packed again and joined his mother, his sister Dora and the Wyndowe children, and also Thersie and her daughter Florence, in Weston. This was a large family gathering. The first evening there he went with his mother to a lecture on those ever popular Victorian subjects, craniology, phrenology and mesmerism.

Next morning he bathed from a machine, discovering later that the custom in Weston was for men to undress on the beach and run down to the sea naked. This he did next day giving a free rein to his libido: "There was a delicious feeling of freedom in stripping in the open air and running down naked to the sea, where the waves were curling white with foam and the red morning sunshine glowing upon the naked limbs of the bathers."

He made a trip alone to Glastonbury and Wells, and a few days later went with his mother on a paddle steamer to Ilfracombe. The sea was rough and he noted the quiet that fell upon the fellow passengers all arrayed in finery. Then as the sea grew choppier Kilvert with that superiority that claims all good sailors began to look humorously at the others. With irony he quotes Byron: "A change came o'er the spirit of the dream", and he views the sick leaning over the gunwale "as if they were engaged in private prayer or in some act of worship to the sea". Only he and his mother seemed to enjoy the motion, though Mrs Kilvert was disturbed by the water swilling over the deck.

When the party broke up, Kilvert journeyed down to Taunton where the Hockins had moved. He enjoyed their company and especially that of his godchild Beatrice. On his return journey he thought of the happy family, and it is not fanciful to see the envy he felt when he looked at those sharing his compartment "a good-humoured sleepy Irish Squire and a family of the fairest noblest looking boys I ever saw, travelling with a dark-bearded father and a fair noble-looking mother".

Back at the rectory he was in family life once more, and the diary entries are on the whole shorter. Life was different, and he had more demands upon his time in the house and garden. One evening he carried pots of cuttings round from the stable yard into the stone court, "an Herculean labour my mother said".

Back in England he returned to a very definite place in the structure of English society. He was not just 'the curate of Clyro', however popular and likeable he may have been in that role. In Langley he was not only a parson and the son of the vicar known to the district for a long time. He was also the grandson of Squire Coleman and related to the Ashes at the 'big house'.

All this is evident in his contact with the people. There is not the same easy encounter; rather, there is a very English tinge of respect and knowledge of one's place. This comes out in a visit he made with his father to Box to visit Jerry Knight who was in a private mental home. Kilvert calls it, more bluntly, an Asylum. "The unfortunate Knight, suffering from delusions and having a fear of poisons, was starving himself. He was pleased, as many mad and sad people were, to see Kilvert and instantly he called him 'Mr Frank'." It was the old respect mixed with a shy familiarity.

Kilvert's place in local society is even more definitely underlined when, with his mother, he takes tea with some genteel old ladies in Chippenham and the conversation was of their kinsfolk and genealogy. Even the drive there had stirred memories of his childhood when he saw Hardenhuish Rectory "where we were all born". He thought that he almost heard the voices of the boys of the past who had played in Alington Meads. These meetings with the past were not all pleasant. He went with a distant cousin to Langley House to show her the ancestral portraits, and one was of Madam Ashe. This aroused the diarist's antipathy: "Of my great grandmother's picture I have a peculiar hatred". The stories recounted in the family of this lady were all of a hard, self-willed and unloving woman. Even when out to supper his host, Mr Woods, talks of Kilvert's family and tells him how his great grandfather had sold a farm to his grandfather. He speaks of the immense coach that Squire Ashe had built when he was High Sheriff of the County and he ends with a phrase about Langley House: "there was no such pride as there is now". The proximity of Langley House and the autocracy of the squire was to provide the bacterium in the milk that was to turn the whole sour.

It was inevitable and it was not unexpected. But for the time it was hidden. Kilvert began making improvements to the church and to the house. With his father he screwed brass candle sconces to the pulpit. Out in the stable he cleaned the brass and polished the leather of the harness, making it shine brighter than it had for years. Pleased with his work he drives to the station to meet his mother. Alas, she fails to notice the splendour of the equipage, for she was more concerned that her pocket had been picked in Bath and she had lost ten shillings.

The family idyll continues. Father reads aloud from *Lorna Doone*, and Kilvert buys a nine foot long bagatelle board. The silver cup given him in Clyro he takes to be engraved with the Kilvert crest and coat of arms and, like a true Victorian, he cannot resist additional adornment and has the motto 'Pergrinamus' placed beneath the scallop shells. In those early months at Langley there are three references to church matters which throw some light on the attitudes of both Kilvert clergymen. The young man is upset to see the black wine bottle placed at the Communion service on the altar. It should, of course, have been on the credence table and, better still, it should not have been a bottle but a flagon of glass, or silver. It is an indication of how the standards of the old man were slipping as he grew weary. Another incident arose from the fact that the Oxford Movement, which had sprung from his college, Oriel, had not affected him deeply. High churchmen, which the Oxford movement were, kept the anniversaries of their ordination. It was not until the family were all at supper one evening that the old man reminds them that forty years before on that day he had been ordained and preached his first sermon. These were the rather casual attitudes into which Kilvert had been born.

Kilvert's delight was to have all done with decency, order and beauty. The church with its hierarchy, its meetings and jostling for place and power did not draw him at all. When he went to a clergy and laity conference in Bristol, he met friends and acquaintances, but after lunch the lovely autumn weather tempted him to "cut the afternoon . . . , it seemed a pity to sit in a stuffy room any longer. So I mouched and stealing down Park St. unobserved I breathed freely again in College Green". There he felt much happier unbothered by argument, or the necessity of concentrating and making decisions about matters which were of comparatively little importance to him. He looked around the cathedral and knelt where he had been ordained. He went down the hill and "paid a flying visit to the glorious Church of St. Mary Redcliffe at last completed by a noble spire. Poor Chatterton. Poor Chatterton". This serves to remind us that poetry had, I feel, an equal place in his reverence and devotion. His sympathies would be with the boy Chatterton who had to go to such lengths of forgery to get his work seen. A little later he met Miss Mewburn who showed him a pamphlet about the possibility that the British were the living descendants of the lost ten tribes of Israel. The linking of religion and romantic history and patriotism stirred him: the idea appealed immensely: "It would be a glorious truth".

No more is heard of the British Israelites, but we do hear of Miss Mewburn's indignation. She attended an agricultural meeting in Chippenham Town Hall where the poor and the old labourers were kept standing whilst 'their betters' sat on padded chairs during patronising speeches. Kilvert shared her feelings, for he was aware that he had returned to a class system which, at times, seemed not so much class as caste. But there was still the charm of being at home and surrounded by thoughtfulness and affection: "I came up by the midnight mail and reached Langley at 2.30 a.m. When I came in I found a fire in my bedroom, the kettle singing on the hob, and a strange but comfortable armchair, and sandwiches, sherry and sugar on the table". This was a wonderful improvement on lodgings where they let the fire die out and the carpet was dirty.

It is very easy, comparing the lyricism of the diary of the Border Country with the less rapturous entries in Langley Burrell, to view the latter as a place of constraint and frustration. That was not so. In some ways Kilvert realised here part of his priestly vocation far better. It is not difficult to see that his father had come to Langley a tired man. There had been the constant vigilance needed being a schoolmaster, and one must remember too the very short holidays they then had. With the boys perpetually around him Robert Kilvert was worn out. Then he had met constantly with opposition from Squire Ashe when any change was mooted. The old man had given up the struggle. His inability to cope is revealed in little things. When Kilvert and Dora decorated the church for a wedding on New Year's Day 1873, they found: "The red altar cloth was edged with a double border of ivy leaves, which partly concealed its scanty dimensions and its sad moth-eaten state. Mary Knight was shocked, and she said she would prepare her brother Jacob, the parish Churchwarden, for a demand for a new altar cloth".

Later in January Kilvert goes to Langley House "to beard the lion in his den". There was finance to be discussed and the Squire, evidently wary of the young curate's enthusiasm, "begged that the Church should not be washed with yellow ochre". But Kilvert gained his consent that Holy Communion should be conducted from the altar and not the reading desk. He gained an ally in Mrs Ashe and it was conceded that two chairs should be placed within the chancel. It must have been a grudging consent, for the stubborn fellow added that he did not like "the idea of a clergyman sitting within the rails during the service and thought that he should not 'lounge' in a chair".

Kilvert also had a confirmation class that gave him immense satisfaction, and when the day came for the bishop to perform the service he described the day as being one of the happiest in his life. He was pleased with the entire occasion because it was "nice and quiet, no hurry, confusion or excitement and the behaviour of all the young pupils was quiet and reverent in the extreme. It made me very happy to see them".

The bishop stayed at the 'big house' and the Kilverts were probably suspicious of what the squire was telling him. The bishop was probably well aware of the tensions between the houses; it was a common nineteenth century phenomenon, and when the families were related it was invariably worse. When the bishop viewed the church "he allowed that throughout the whole Church there was a ray of amelioration". The squire was difficult, but at the time it may only have added a certain piquancy to Kilvert's task, and a certain sense of triumph must have been his when an obstacle was overcome. Kilvert was assuming many of the responsibilities of his father. This added to his confidence and was in many ways an excellent preparation for the day when he would have a parish of his own.

By temperament Kilvert was a contented man and, for a diarist, singularly without introspection. He did not question himself, and was amazingly unquestioning about his faith, this to a degree almost disturbing to a clergyman of the latter part of the twentieth century. This contentment is apparent in an entry for September 1873. After spending time helping his father pick and store apples he writes:

> In the afternoon as I was sitting under the shade of the acacia on the lawn enjoying the still warm sunshine of the holy autumn day it was a positive luxury to be alive. A tender haze brooded melting over the beautiful landscape, and the peaceful silence was only broken by the chuckling and grumbling of a squirrel leaping among the acacia boughs overhead, and the clear sweet solitary notes of a robin singing from the copper beech.

It seems the very essence of mid-Victorian middle-class life. It is the peaceful, leisured picture of a vicarage afternoon which lingers erroneously in the minds of many even for present day clergy. It was a moment; it was a fleeting flash of time caught by Kilvert. Those are the moments he was so acute to record and which make him so valuable.

Yet the very next day he rose early and he met Herriman, a railway porter, returning from his night shift. He ponders on the difference in their lives and how he, the diarist, has so much more enjoyment and leisure. He knows that the porter has only three days holiday in the year while Kilvert himself usually took, on average, ten weeks. The serious and fair minded priest wrote: "And for no desert of mine. Surely there will be compensation made for these things hereafter if not here".

In the middle of the last century there was increasing awareness of the injustices in the prevailing social order, but to the comfortable middle classes, especially in the country, it was a thought to be shunned rather than cherished. Kilvert considered these things not because he was anything of a social theorist but because he talked and visited and, much more important, listened to the people, particularly the poor, and the deprived. They aroused his compassion. So he listened to the family gardener and handyman John Couzens, a loyal but occasionally obsequious servant, who spoke his thoughts to his younger master as he never would the older. One day, fork in his hand, he said: "I know it's coming, as sure as this prong is in my hand". What was prophesied was of course revolution. In fact rebellion was deflected into imperialism and a new patriotism — which Kilvert did not live to experience — with Queen Victoria emerging from the widowed shadows to be well-nigh deified at her Jubilees.

Kilvert's gift was sensibility and an ability to see beneath the surface of things when others were dazzled by the outward show.

In Bath he saw a circus procession of some size and magnificence. Kilvert sees the tawdry tinsel, the coarse-looking dirty woman and most of all the wretchedness of "a poor pale thin girl with a flood of yellow hair and a worn anxious face with a terrified unhappy look that went to one's heart". She was dressed as an angel and stood precariously on a pedestal on the top of a lofty cart. Kilvert, it seems, had heart, he had imagination and he loved children.

In Langley he had easier access to a wider world than he had had in Clyro. One example of this was the great Church Congress in Bath in 1873, the reason for Kilvert's visit to that city. The work of such men as Charles Kingsley and Frederick Dennison Maurice was bearing fruit and Christian Socialism was becoming a factor to be reckoned with. The congress he attended gripped his attention and this time he did not mouch away. It was very largely devoted to a discussion of the Church's attitudes towards strikes and the rightful use of labour. Audiences were told, and not merely by the forceful but also by bishops, that to strike may be perfectly legitimate, and they were asked "Can we conceive St. James or St. Paul taking the side of the upper classes against the lower?" These were new and revolutionary ideas and Kilvert for all his sympathy had never asked these questions. Indeed he had inveighed against a miner's strike in a belligerent and uninformed way.

On the Episcopal Bench at that time was James Frazer, Bishop of Manchester. He had been described as "the Citizen-Bishop, the lawn-sleeved citizen". In 1873 the French Revolution was of course still less than a hundred years into the past, and the word 'citizen' still held vibrations of the Terror. A year later this same bishop was to arbitrate between the master painters and their workforce. His decision was accepted. Ideas of freedom and the rights of labour were in the air and Kilvert was perhaps affected. Typically he picked out the stirring and poetic phrases of a sermon: "natural laws are not chains bound about the living God, but threads which He holds in His hand". He was stirred by the surge of mainly manly voices in the great congregation reciting the General Confession.

Very humanly in the midst of higher challenging thoughts, Eros planted a beautiful young girl in a long grey cloak in his vision. He watched her intently, enchanted by her "shower of golden-brown hair". Her gentle humble attitude in prayer roused purer responses: "In the perpetual struggle between the powers and principles of good and evil the obesiance rebuked and put to flight an evil thought". He was very much flesh and blood and cruelly denied marriage.

This rallying of great ideals of the Church Militant was good for him and must have helped him when he was back again in the small world of the parish. He was having to consult the squire again, for the Archbishop of Canterbury had recommended a Special Day of Prayer for Missionaries. It so happened neither Kilvert nor his father were in favour of this. The squire agreed, but in his peppery way was more emphatic: "he objected to Revivals and all such spasmodic efforts and thought that our regular services were sufficient. The thing was, he believed, to infuse more life and vigour into them. He spoke about the singing [the war whoop], the new stove pipe, and Annie Hawkins' grave. Was it deep enough?" and he considered having mixed audiences at evening lectures in the winter unadvisable. Sweethearts would be together on moonlit nights.

It is easy to see the powerful parishioner grumbling about the services, when at the same time he vigorously opposes anything done to improve them. He harks back to his own obsessions, the heating of the church, the depth of the graves. All this is familiar stuff to many country parsons even today. But perhaps few today have a squire so insensitive as to measure graves whilst the bereaved were in the church, and who "on a cold day ordered the schoolmistress to open all the windows". Ashe was a bully. Kilvert's dislike is obvious when he describes the squire in a white hat cantering his bay pony across the park at the phalanx of his daughters in a line before the house, "his usual joke. The infantry scattered right and left" by the cavalry.

The mean triviality of all this seemed far from the stirring messages of the Congress. But Kilvert had not forgotten. He was not a man for meetings, his gift was in his contact with ordinary working people at a deep level. For instance here was an old man called Benjamin, who had some claim to being a mystic. One night in January 1874 Kilvert took him a present of a large printed book. He found the old man reading a book of sermons aloud to himself. It hapened to be the eve of the old man's seventy-fifth birthday. Benjamin talked of his deceased wife and he confided in Kilvert that:

> 'I think the Lord has made her a doorkeeper. She is keeping the door for me. I saw her in a vision of the night. It was not a dream, and I could see her long white robe down to her feet. When I go I think she will open the door to me and go further in, and then I shall keep the door for someone else. I never told any one about it before for fear of raising a laugh.'
>
> 'You have beautiful thoughts, Benjamin,' I said. 'I think God must put them into your mind.' 'I know Satan doesn't put them there' said the old man.

He told Kilvert of another vision. He saw a shop full of dresses. Some were brown for work and others were white for heaven. A boy in tattered clothes came in and wanted a brown dress. Kilvert rashly gave an explanation: "The shop meant the world and the boy was just born into it". "'Yes,' said the old man, 'or he was born for heaven". It is good to observe Kilvert's sensitive acceptance of the old man's tale. Too often such tales are dismissed, or as the old man feared, laughed at.

Then there was the occasion when one misty night he met George Bourchier much the worse for drink. "'George', I said sadly and gently, 'you have had too much.' 'I have sir. God forgive me. I cry about it night and morning. I will try to leave it off. God bless you.'" Kilvert the shepherd comments, "The poor wandering sheep".

One of the coldest, longest and most painful jobs on the land for children was bird-scaring. A picture by Sir George Clausen in Preston Art Gallery captures not only the cold, the weariness of the boy who stands in the smoke of a meagre fire, but the utter loneliness as well. Richard Jefferies understood this unwanted solitude: he mentions a boy who crossed a vast downland field just to see him as he walked by and to hear a human voice. Kilvert also captures this: "A bird-tenting boy with a light heart was singing at the top of his voice across the fields . . . . When he had ended his song the boy relieved his feelings by a shout and then sang 'Saturday night is soon a coming'."

The revolution John Couzens had foretold never came, at least not bloodily, to Britain. One possible factor is not hard to find. Britain had many clergymen like Kilvert, and every village and every town had its crowd of unmarried and unoccupied young women. They filled their lives with good works, teaching in schools and Sunday schools and visiting the sick. It is not often noted, but the world Kilvert describes is much akin to the country houses of Chekhov's plays and the labouring people and peasants to the characters of his stories. In Russia, particularly in the rural areas, the church was basically a peasant institution, visited somewhat aloofly by the gentry on their periodic residence at the big house. Richard Lister Venables had noted this in his book on Russia before Chekhov was born. He, too, foresaw calamity. There was not in Russia the link between the classes that the church provided in Britain enabling a greater understanding often, though not always, between them. Possibly people like the Kilverts, the Venables, the Thomas girls, the Dew family and the Ashe girls (one became a committed Socialist councillor in Southwark) played some part in staving off the catastrophe of a great revolution.

Kilvert must not be considered a far-sighted socialist. He often reverted to type and resented change and the threatening of his own privileges. He shows this one day when he sees a carriage pulled by greys with a postillion spanking along the road. It was a wedding carriage, and he then remembers a nearby farmer's marriage: "There is no holding these yeomen now. Here was a case of 8 bridesmaids". He had forgotten that the mud on our boots is not far distant from most of us.

There was a tranquillity in Kilvert, however. It was partly temperament, partly his belief, and this with his Wordsworthian awareness enabled him to look, to pause, to give thanks and write about it. The familiar wooded garden around the rectory, something seen so often, so familiar that he could have been forgiven for overlooking it, aroused this picture of the end of a day on the eve of May:

> As the evening sunlight shone bright and searching across the lawn upon the lime the shadows of the leaves were cast strongly upon the tree trunk. The leaves were so brilliant that even their shadows showed a pale faint ghostly green. The shadow looked like the spirits of leaves without the body.

Kilvert, who loved pictures, particularly those that told a story, could make his pen paint an Impressionist picture. Quite unconsciously he knew, like the artists, that shadows were not black. Yet one knows that had he been confronted by a Manet he would have found it hard to like. To him it would have appeared unfinished. But it was good that he had these moments of vision, for life was to become increasingly and irritatingly difficult.

The harmony of the church in Langley Burrell was always a frail component in its character. In the autumn of 1874 there was a storm and, as in most crises, the catalyst was a small one and most ironically a harmonium. That so humble an instrument, one which has never achieved distinction in musicians' estimation, should have wrought such mischief is comic to us. It is an episode that can be read with merriment. It can very validly be placed alongside Hardy's humorous mastepiece about the village choir in *Under the Greenwood Tree*.

It all began with the imperious dismissal of the old leader of the singing in church, George Jefferies. A note from the squire informed the vicarage that he had spoken to Jefferies, saying that he would no longer pay for his services and that he hoped that he had not hurt the old man's feelings by saying that he had made the service "not only ridiculous but laughed at." Tact had never been an asset owned by the squire. Perhaps he had rarely had to use it. It meant that, not before time, the church had to lurch into the contemporary method of accompanying the singing; an organ or a harmonium.

The Kilvert family was, in fact, more hurt than the old leader of music. They had not been consulted, and their authority and responsibility had been contemptuously affronted. Kilvert was furious and all the buried rage of months boiled up in a seething paragraph. "We are prepared to give up the living and leave the place should we be obliged to do so rather than submit any longer to this tyranny". Sadly he adds: "I don't think it will come to this. No such luck to leave Langley. We should all be better and happier elsewhere, more independent and what is most important of all we should have more self-respect. For my own part I should for many reasons be glad and thankful to go. I don't know how it will end. I suppose I shall stay here as long as my father lives, no longer".

A harmonium was borrowed and placed at the rear of the church. On All Hallowmass day, "Fanny played the harmonium nicely and the singing was capital". The people generally were delighted; it was a great improvement on the uncertain quavers of George Jefferies. Plans were set afoot to buy a new one. Dora, the one with the most spirit in the family, went to Langley House to ask Mr Ashe to head the subscription list. He replied very trenchantly that neither he nor anyone of his household would give as much as a farthing.

One evening Kilvert walked home with a parishioner who gave voice to the ground swell of opinion. "'Oh' she said earnestly . . . .'oh, it's a comfort to know that there's a time coming when no one will be able to reign over us and when we shall be as good as those who are so high and proud over us now'." The subscriptions rolled in. It was not music alone that they were supporting, it was rebellion. Before November was out the new harmonium from Weymouth had been installed and all paid for. The squire, angry and embittered at being 'bested', behaved very ungraciously. He complained generally and on a raw, foggy and frosty November Sunday entered the church. When he smelt that the stove had been lit, he turned and left hastily. His wife and daughter remained and, embarrassed and eager to make amends, spoke kindly of Fanny's playing of the new instrument.

Naturally not all their emotions or energy had been engaged in this little war, but misery had been felt by many. Three weeks later Kilvert took a party of children to Chippenham to see a magic lantern lecture on the journeys of David Livingstone, which they loved; and he writes, "What pleasure these few pence have given to twenty-one young hearts. How easy it is to make people happy". No comparison is drawn explicitly, but it is there. Weeks later Kilvert talked with one of the churchwardens and the topic of the harmonium came up. The warden said that he was pleased in the way it had been procured, and what pleased him most was "independence".

Kilvert himself at this time was not happy. He was frustrated in many ways and he needed independence himself. When his pony was refractory and would not let itself be harnessed, he seized the broom and belaboured the animal until the broomhead flew off. His father needed him, he was increasingly deaf, and at meetings Kilvert made notes so that his father could know what was being said. Their lack of funds and a certain timidity hampered them. He wrote: "Our tenure of this living is a very precarious one", and with even greater bitterness he added, "it is the warm nest on the rotten bough".

# 15.

# Kilvert and the Arts

All his life, it would seem, Kilvert aspired to be a poet. At one point he belonged to the Harrow Weald Poetical Society. A contemporary list of the twenty members has both Kilvert and his brother Edward amongst them. He was by no means ashamed of his poetry, for he read it to friends and parishioners and gave a manuscript copy to Ettie Meredith Brown. He wished to publish it but his father was not at all encouraging, and there is mention of a courteous but discouraging letter from Longmans, the publishers. After Kilvert's death the poems were published privately by his widow, called *Musings in Verse*.

William Plomer, writing in the introduction, says succinctly and truly: "His poems are not comparable with his prose and show the typical weaknesses of mid-Victorian verse. They help to illustrate the working of Kilvert's mind and the nature of his sentiments". The poems reveal the truth of this man who was so much a man of his time; often very conventional, with copy-book morals. They are like so much verse of his time, and indeed, later, unappetisingly moral. The best known and even loved poem of his is called 'Honest Work.' He had this printed on cards and distributed, many of which were treasured after his death and, such is the oddity of criticism of poetry, considered good by often intelligent people.

'Honest Work' in its beginning is composed of short couplets:

> Honest work is always holy
> Howsoever hard and lowly
>
> In the milking of the cows,
> In the sweeping of the house,
> In the following of the plough,
> In the lopping of the bough,
> In the tending of the sheep,
> There are meanings, sacred, deep.

113

For a moment one thinks that it is going to be reminiscent of George Herbert, but alas, sentimentality creeps in and there is a lack of originality.

The poems that appeal are about the countryside he knew and its people and incidents we have already encountered in the diary. His poem on little Davie is a poetic version of the death of the shepherd's son as told him by the grieving mother. It does move one, but not as strongly as the prose version. In his verse he was hampered by tradition and knowledge so that he writes following a precedent rather than striking a spark from his own soul. He is strangely lacking in metaphors or invention. Plomer's words are again apt and clear: "it is easy to point out the limitations of Kilvert's poeticising . . . those who best understand and appreciate his character may find it reflected in his verse, interestingly and sometimes touchingly." Most of the verse was written in his happy period in Clyro when he was young, fairly untroubled, deeply satisfied in his ministry and when he still had not felt the blows life so often inflicts.

After his death a poem was found in his blotter entitled 'Nydd Eos', which in Welsh strictly should be 'Nydd yr Eos', meaning 'The Nest of the Nightingale'. I had cause to read this poem to a group of people in the great Walk of Monnington. I warned them that it was not very good poetry; it was Tennysonian without the magic, or so I thought. As I read I became aware of the intent listening; they found magic and at the end there was that curious corporate sigh which occurs, usually, only when good poetry is heard. I for one think it was a combination of the words and Kilvert's life.

He was writing of himself, he likened himself to the nightingale. It must have been written after Katharine Heanley broke their engagement, when he was low and depressed. He speaks glancingly of Langley Burrell, Clyro, St. Harmons and now his home by the river. He foresees death in the last stanza:

> Let him sing a little while in peace, his songs will soon be o'er,
> And the singer speed his wings with joy to find a happier shore,
> When the nest is found forsaken, some will smile and some will
> sigh,
> For the voice which now no longer mingles with the murmuring
> Wye.

114

He had a gift, but it was not his greatest gift; that was prose to celebrate the day, and one of the days he celebrated was a visit to William Barnes, the Dorset poet. This diary entry has unconsciously so many twists that it does become a piece of prose poetry.

On 30th April 1874 Kilvert rose early and left Chippenham on the 7.15 train. He was in a bright anticipatory mood and was met at Dorchester by Henry Moule the vicar of Fordington, a contemporary of Kilvert's father. Together the two clergymen walked through the town and Kilvert noted the avenues of sycamores and chestnut which still lend such enchantment to this town. Beneath the trees he noted "a lovely girl dressed in deep mourning and walking with her lover, probably a bold handsome artilleryman from the barracks, splendid in blue and gold". Dorchester, Hardy, and one wonders momentarily if Kilvert had stumbled upon Bathsheba Everdene and Sergeant Troy. He was, anyway seeing exactly what Hardy often saw and which fuelled his mighty and often sardonic imagination.

The vicar talked of his troubled life as he had striven to improve Fordington, working to have some races stopped which each year brought a flood of bad characters to the town and which always left a rich crop of illegitimate children nine months later. Moule was very much a man with a mission and he had struggled against the fierce opposition of vested interests, one of them being The Duchy of Cornwall. It was an admirable, even heroic story, but not unfamiliar. Many vicars in Victorian England fought such battles. Like Moule they often won and became revered and respected.

At last they reached the thatched rectory of Winterbourne Came, so rustic a house with its gothic windows and thatched verandah running all round that it looked, and looks still, more like a little house of Staffordshire china than a real house. From the verandah came the poet Barnes, excusing his almost unique garb, as picturesque as his house: "He wore a dark grey loose gown girt round the waist with a black cord and tassel, black knee breeches, black silk stockings and gold buckled shoes". The bald head, the silvery hair and long white beard impressed the younger man and he saw the mixture of benevolence and keen intelligence: "He is a very remarkable, and a very remarkable-looking man, half hermit, half enchanter".

Kilvert told him of his frequent reading of his poems and his deep admiration. The old man was pleased and told him of his writing, always using known places, known characters from his past. He lifted a character from one village to another, placed a river near a town where in fact no water was. This was the active imagination at work. He warmed to Kilvert and told him of his second sight about a house and its children.

Moule, whose son Horace had committed suicide the previous autumn, had written a poem in his unhappiness beginning: "Lord I love thee". He had written music to accompany this verse, and sitting at the piano he played and sang, so impressing Kilvert that he calls him "a universal genius". Then the real poet was called to read and his tale of the Miller visiting the Crystal Palace had them all in roars of laughter. At this point Kilvert did what poets love most; he asked for specific poems. Later they talked of philology and of the cattle calls of Dorset and Wiltshire which were of Scandinavian origin; a subject to delight the diarist.

Walking back with Moule, Kilvert listened to this earnest Evangelical talk once more of his parish, and he was again both interested and a little awed. Henry Moule was a forceful man and he produced equally endowed sons. One became curator of the Dorset County Museum and a painter of water-colours recording the landscape of Hardy's novels. Another became Bishop of Durham, yet another the head of a Cambridge college, and the rest workers in the Church and Mission Field. But it is Horace, the sad tormented man, who claims fame, mainly because he was a mentor to the young Thomas Hardy. He introduced Hardy to reading he might not have stumbled upon alone. Hardy followed Moule, and was left shorn of all his beliefs. Kilvert was but one man away from meeting Hardy. Moule could have made the introduction. It is a fascinating surmise. Yet Kilvert never mentions *Far from the Madding Crowd* which appeared that very year.

There is only one regret in this passage, for one has the impression that the voluble Mr Moule by his talk blunted some of the sharpness of the impression Barnes had made. It is almost as if religion ousted poetry, and that precisely is what undermined most of Kilvert's poetry, conventional piety being a soft centre to his verse. Whereas there is something Spartan, mysterious and real, in the diary entry "An angel satyr walks these hills; it has a religion of its own".

One of Kilvert's poems is called 'Faithful Unto Death' and is obviously based on Sir Edwin Poynter's famous picture of the Roman sentinel on guard whilst Vesuvius erupts and engulfs the city. It is, once again, a poem with an heroic theme, that of unquestioning devotion to duty. Kilvert was moved and his poem ends: "And he still he moved our souls to tears, Who stood on guard a thousand years".

Poynter's soldier joined with Kilvert's verse leads us to think of the diarist's attitude to painting. He enjoyed pictures and he often went to the Royal Academy and other galleries, sharing a general interest of the middle-classes to which he so thoroughly belonged. The Victorian home whether rich or poor, palace or cottage, was decked with pictures, and a house without any was deemed mean and miserable. To analyse Kilvert's reactions is interesting but not entirely merited, for his response to art was not a matter of major importance to him. It was much more a subject for conversation by a fireside with friends, but it has become petrified in the written word.

Rosalind Billingham has pointed out that he could so easily have seen some of the Impressionists at the Paul Durand-Ruel gallery in New Bond Street. Indeed he could, but like many others he did not, so the gallery closed after a comparatively short time. Had he seen them it is safe to hazard that he would not have liked them. He would have thought them crude and unfinished. Yet he frequently saw with the eye of an Impressionist. The entry for 7th October 1874 links him with the French 'pleinairistes':

> For some time I have been trying to find the right word for the shimmering glancing twinkling movement of the poplar leaves in the sun and wind. This afternoon I saw the word written on the poplar leaves. It was 'dazzle'. The dazzle of the poplars.

But the real key word in Kilvert's appreciation is the adjective 'pretty'. He required and expected something pleasing. As Rosalind Billingham points out very pertinently, Kilvert, like most amateurs, was uninhibited in his appreciation of the great masters. Old time had confirmed his new opinion, so he was safe. He found Cuyp, Potter, Rubens and Van Dyck easy to admire.

At Dulwich in June 1876 he saw Murillo's famous smiling girl, 'The Flower Seller', and he really loved "Rembrandt's immortal servant girl [who] still leaned on her round white arms a-smiling from the window as she has leaned and smiled for three hundred years since that summer's day when her master drew her portrait and made her immortal, imperishable and ever young".

But it is still Murillo who excites the longest passage on any picture. It is 'The Good Shepherd', a child guiding two lambs:

> The child's eyes are uplifted and in them and over his whole face there is a marvellous beauty. An indescribable look of heavenly light and purity and an expression in which are blended sweetness and trust, resignation and love. The Good Shepherd whilst guiding his lambs looks upward for guidance himself. No words can do justice to or convey an adequate impression of this extraordinary picture.

The words betray the thought. His Victorian religion is deeply involved here, and sweetness, trust, resignation and love are frequent words in nineteenth century piety.

In any picture Kilvert first sought the subject and preferably this had to be a human figure conveying emotion. It could also however be an animal; a dog arousing pathos or a stag with nobility in its bearing. Therefore, like Queen Victoria, he admired Landseer. It would seem that unlike the Prince Consort he did not care for Italian Primitives, but he would have agreed with the Prince that "Turner was mad".

It is really surprising that Lady Butler, who began her career as Elizabeth Thompson, did not move him. Her 'Roll Call', a scene after a battle in the Crimean War, was a sensation at the Academy in 1874. The crush to see it was so great that a policeman was placed on duty by it, who, as Kilvert comments, said continually "Move on, ladies. Ladies, move on." Kilvert had heard much about the picture and his initial feeling was disappointment. He had expected something larger. All he could say of it was that it was striking. The present writer spent much of his time looking at an engraving of this picture hanging on a dormitory wall. It was his last vision at night and it was still there when he awoke. It aroused in him the uneasy partners of patriotism and pacifism. He admired the courage, cameraderie, the compassion of the older soldier for a battle shocked boy. He felt bitterly for the wounds and the utter weariness. Not until forty years had passed did he see the original and all his old emotions flooded back, but fired and renewed by the sombre emotive colours. It is strange that Kilvert did not see this.

There is no doubt that Kilvert liked both the pretty, the appealing and the slightly erotic, and if combined with religion so much the better. He brought for his friends the Hockins a copy of 'Clinging to the Cross' or 'Rock of Ages'. This was painted by J.A. Dertal, a German-born American. It depicts a draped maiden in a turbulent sea clinging to a rock roughly shaped like a cross. The miracle is that the nubile maiden under such trying circumstances manages to keep her luxuriantly curled and waved hair completely dry. This picture sold in thousands and became a favourite in cottages at the turn of the century.

The most telling thing of all concerning Kilvert's appreciation of art is the entry for 27th May 1876. He went to the Taylor Galleries in Oxford with his friend Mayhew, ostensibly to look at Turner's watercolours of Oxford. They go unmentioned.

> We fell into talk with the Keeper who was formerly a Light Dragoon and rode in the Charge at Balaclava. He was very anxious to go to London to see some pictures of the famous Light Cavalry Charge which he had heard are now on view. 'I could get the time' he said, but added sadly, ' cannot afford to go'. We thought it hard that a man who had helped make history should not see the picture of the history he had made, so we started a little subscription to make up 15/- to send the old soldier to London.

People were foremost in Kilvert's affections. People were more important than ideas.

That same day he passed the shop of Hill and Saunders. "I stopped to take a long last lingering look and farewell of the beautiful Slave Girl". Four days later he took that picture to Bath to be framed. It is to be hoped that 'L'Esclave', or 'The Slave Girl' will one day be recognised and we can see the object of his admiration. Rosalind Billingham acutely summarizes Kilvert's attitude to the arts:

> Kilvert's were the tastes of a warm-blooded and observant young man. He revealed little soul-searching or mental conflict in his

writing, and he did not seek interpretations of these states of mind in the arts. Yet his preferences reflect the values of Victorian society. His choices reflect piety, patriotism, and the English love of animals and children. We should look elsewhere for formal analysis and stylistic criticism.

# 16.

# "A Lover With Disaster On His Face."

Adelaide Cholmeley, the third daughter of Francis Kilvert of Claverton Lodge, uncle and headmaster of the diarist, came up to Langley Burrell with her daughter Addie on 17th July 1874. The following month Addie was to marry Charles Heanley and all the preparations and anticipations were in hand for the marriage. One is a little suspicious as to why Adelaide and her daughter made this special visit to Langley. It is possible that the family were anxious to find a wife for Frank Kilvert. Furthermore Addie knew of her future sister-in-law's unhappy love affair: therefore mother and daughter thought as Victorian ladies did (and indeed many since) that a marriage might well be, if not arranged, then set in motion between Katharine and Kilvert. So they pressed a rather reluctant Kilvert into accepting the invitation to the wedding in August at Findon, a village close to Worthing in Sussex.

The disinclined diarist reveals his lack of enthusiasm when in the train he answered a clergyman who asked him, as they drew near to Portsmouth, if he were going to the Island (Isle of Wight): "No, I wish I were". In the diary he adds, "little knowing what I was saying, or what was in store for me at Findon. How blind we are and unable to see a step before us".

He drove to lodgings in Worthing and went for a walk. The sea seemed too rough for bathing. Looking back he regrets that he did not visit his cousins and so meet Katharine Heanley before the wedding. For the wedding day entry opens with: "This may be one of the happiest and most important days in my life, for today I fell in love at first sight with sweet Kathleen Mavourneen". This was Kilvert's name for Katharine Heanley. How prophetic was his unusually cautious use of the subjunctive mood. The day remained happy but the consequences were to be intolerably sad.

It was an extremely pretty wedding in the attractive Sussex church with its many pointed gables and spire. School children, "South Saxons" as Kilvert calls them, "were lined on the churchyard path dressed all alike in white frocks, broad white straw hats trimmed with white and rose colour, a breast knot of scarlet geranium, and each had a nosegay of flowers to throw in the bride's path". It was a cherubic picture; some of the infantine faces might have served as models to Correggio.

The bridesmaids numbered five and there was a groomsman appointed to escort each of them. Sarah Cholmeley pointed Kilvert's out to him: "there is your bridesmaid, the tall dark one behind on the right hand side". The girls all came up and were introduced. Kilvert wrote,

> a tall handsome girl with very dark hair, eyebrows and eyelashes, and beautiful bright grey eyes, a thin high aristocratic nose, a sweet firm rosy mouth, beautiful white teeth, a well developed chin, a clear complexion and fresh colour. That was Kathleen Mavourneen as I first saw her. I noticed afterwards that she wore pearl earrings.

There is, I feel something of assessment in this list of her physical attributes, even a hint of criticism in a "well developed chin". It is true that he had already said that he had fallen in love at first sight, but that was a somewhat common experience with Kilvert. I cannot but feel that this is a man talking himself into love with a comely, attractive young woman who is very suitable, rather than being swept along by emotion.

The wedding was more than usually tribal. One Cholmeley uncle, Dr Robert, performed the marriage ceremony, another uncle led the bride up the aisle because her brother was on crutches. After the wedding ceremony most of the party went up to the top of Chanctonbury Ring. This height has vast views which stretched that day over the fields, the bright gold of stubble, the green of pasture and the variegated plain to the grandstand at Epsom. Kilvert was attracted to Katharine and she felt at one with him and they talked of mutual interests, Tennyson's *In Memoriam* being one of them. She spoke of the feeling which many women of her class were acknowledging, the enforced idleness of their lives: "I loved her a hundred times better for her sweet troubled thoughts and honest regretful words".

She told him that she felt that she knew him because Addie had shown her his letters and often spoken to her of him. They were both ready to fall in love; both needed a partner. When they returned to the house she gave him some decorations from the wedding cake and then, unasked, a stephanotis bloom from a bouquet. He vowed in his diary that he would keep it until they were married, or until he was dead.

Jessie Russell, one of the bridesmaids, invited Kilvert to become a member of their Mutual Improvement Society, a typically earnest group of Christian people helping one another. They corresponded and shared poems (some of their own), and by this means Kilvert was able to correspond with Katharine without seeking the formal consent of her parents because it was not of a sentimental nature.

The information we have about Katharine Heanley has been gleaned not ear by ear, but seed by seed by devoted researchers and Eva Farmery in particular. The reason for Katharine's shadowy appearance in the diary is not that Kilvert wrote of her rarely, but because his widow, Elizabeth Rowland, excised nearly all mention of her. However, Elizabeth did leave this rather equivocal description by her husband of the photograph he received from Katharine almost a year after their first meeting: "I thought the face a little stern at first, but when I had looked at it a little time I saw the kindly loving light come into the eyes and the sweet firm mouth begin to smile. This is as it should be. There is no tenderness so beautiful as in the tenderness of strength". He was talking himself into love again, whereas his well-tuned instincts bade him beware, for here was a strength much greater and more dominant than his own.

Katharine Heanley was the daughter of Marshall and Clara Heanley. Heanley was a very successful farmer in Lincolnshire, much respected and sometimes feared. In 1946, fifty years after Heanley's death, an old man said: "A strange man was Marshall Heanley — he could be so hectoring and at other times so kind". Clara, Heanley's second wife, was the daughter of the Reverend and Mrs Robert Cholmeley of Wainfleet in Lincolnshire. Robert Cholmeley was an energetic man who restored his ruinous church, and this energy was not confined to his ministry, for his wife bore fifteen children. Credit must go to her that in an age of high infant mortality, she raised them all to adult life. The Cholmeleys and the Heanleys knew one another from frequent meetings in a sparsely populated area. Coming from a bustling vicarage Clara brought a positive attitude with her, which had been lacking in her unhappy predecessor. She was musical, lively and a good letter-writer, and blessed with a sense of humour, a quality possibly lacking in her husband, and may be in Katharine too.

The Heanleys lived at Bank House Farm on Croft Marsh not far from the then hamlet of Skegness. The farm is a difficult place to find, remotely placed, but in good rich farming soil: Marshall Heanley became a prosperous man together with his brother who farmed nearby. It is a unique area, flat and windy, with vast skyscapes on clear days: it also suffers mists and fogs. It is not a place to be depressed in. The inhabitants say that you either love it, or hate it; there is no intermediate state.

It is now certain that Kilvert visited Croft. He stayed at the vicarage with the Honourable and Reverend Evelyn John Manson and his wife. With them he went to the school and the headmaster recorded the visit in his Log Book. From the vicarage Kilvert must have visited Katharine, but what he wrote in his diary we shall never know. The scissors did their work all too well.

However, Evelyn Manson is important to the story. The arrival in a scattered parish of an eligible young vicar, who was also aristocratic, must have caused many hearts to beat faster and Katharine's was one of them. Katharine fell in love and Manson's flirtatious manner beguiled her, but not her mother. Then suddenly in 1872 Manson married Ann Grace Kinnear, the daughter of a Scottish lawyer. It was a bitter blow to the hopes and desires of Katharine. Years later her cousin made a long story of the romance called 'Bytoft Grange', which was published in 1929 with other stories under the title *The Toll of the Marshes*.

So it is possible to view the love affair of Kilvert and Katharine as the meeting, attraction and hesitant embarkation on a romance between two wounded people. Both had been in love before, both had been hurt. It is a complicated history, partly because so much of the evidence is missing. But it is also further complicated because Kilvert also soon became extremely attached to Ettie Meredith Brown who lived within walking distance of Langley

Burrell Rectory at the beautiful house of 'Nonsuch'. The descriptions of Ettie are rapturous and seem much more spontaneous. There is a real admiration and it is instantaneous:

> She was admirably dressed in light grey with a close fitting body which set off her exquisite figure and suited to perfection her black hair and eyes and her dark Spanish brunette complexion with its rich glow of health which gave her cheeks the dusky bloom and flush of a ripe pomegranate.

She aroused a poetic response in Kilvert. He was always prone to find a source of female attraction close at hand when the real love was far away. It is clear that his passions had been aroused and that on these occasions he became aware of other girls. Richard Holmes finds R.L. Stevenson in similar condition when he is in the Cevennes parted from his future wife and looks amorously at a peasant girl. Holmes describes the condition as being "sexually lonely" which is accurate. So it was Ettie's star that rose and Katharine was temporarily eclipsed.

Kilvert sent his poems to Ettie as an Easter present when the family went to their house in Bournemouth for the spring of 1876. She sent him two sad, sweet verses, one of which began "When shall we meet again?" He wrote that "They were very sweet but very sad and made me feel strangely unhappy".

It was a doomed affair. The family was rich and Kilvert still had no prospects. Furthermore Ettie's father was a Church of England clergyman who had lost his faith, was bitter, and would look most disapprovingly on Kilvert as a suitor on two counts; first, his profession, and secondly his lack of hard cash.

Easter over, Kilvert returned to the Border Country. He went to Monnington-on-Wye to stay with his sister Thersie and her husband William Smith who had recently been appointed rector of that parish. Here he received two letters. There was "a long, sad, sweet loving letter from my darling Ettie, a tender beautiful letter of farewell". With it came a note from her great friend young Mrs Meredith Brown, "friendly and so kind, saying she is afraid Ettie and I must hold no further communication by letter or poetry or any other way. I know it, I know it. She is right and I have been, alas, very very wrong".

Kilvert is both hurt and convicted of behaving foolishly. He was very sad and in the garden of Monnington Rectory he looks at the weeping birch tree, which "wept with me and its graceful drooping tresses softly moving reminded me with a strange sweet thrill of Ettie's hair". The great Scots pines in the famous Walk seemed to sigh with him. Ettie sailed to India and on her arrival married. She lived a conventional life and there were no children.

Four days later Kilvert had a letter from his old rector, Mr Venables, ever a very good, thoughtful and paternal friend. The Archdeacon of Brecon had asked him if Kilvert would consider accepting the living of St Harmon's, a windswept, remote but often beautiful parish about four miles north of Rhayader.

There was, this spring of 1876, an almost frenetic weaving in the romantic and the clerical career of Kilvert. So long his life had seemed a treadmill of duty, though he would never have admitted that. For so long there had been no prospect to look forward to and all plans had been rather nebulous. Suddenly, almost too late, there is hope, and his love returns to Katharine.

Kilvert accepted the living of St Harmon. In his farewell speech at Langley Burrell he spoke of the future partner who would share his joys and sorrows, but did not name her. In the event her story became one of sorrow, darkness, determination and, at the end, deepest despair. Those who see in the diaries only croquet parties, dancing in the drawing room and picnics, who hear only the cooing of the doves in the elms and the gentle crunch of gravel beneath the carriage wheels of callers are wrong. The diaries can be read for nostalgia, but the tragedy should not be ignored. Kilvert pinned down life, and incidentally the lives of those around him. He must be read with imagination. The story that ensues of Katharine is like a novel by the then contemporary realist George Gissing.

As mentioned, Katharine had loved the Hon. Rev. Evelyn Manson but he married another. Her plight was retold by Charlotte Heanley in *The Toll of the Marshes*: the title is significant. The county of Lincolnshire was described to the present writer by a farm-worker as "flat as a penny". This intelligent man could see its loveliness, but he had also experienced its loneliness. He had ploughed, reaped and sown on those endless fields, sometimes seeing nobody and hearing nothing for days. Katharine shared that loneliness. She was in all probability an obsessive young woman,

and had been possessed by her love for Manson. The scattered village of Croft did little to stimulate her intellect or arouse her imagination. In the fine house of her father she would often look out on mist, the sea-fret, of those parts. It made everything grey dull and insubstantial.

Even in her love with Kilvert, he was the second man in her life. Was he ever tactless enough to mention Ettie Meredith Brown? That might confirm a suspicion of fickleness in him and be quite enough to make her withdraw her trust in him. It was a very unhappy situation and the pious young woman carried her fears and apprehensions to the beautiful grey stone church of Croft, going past the Vicarage and the school. These were all reminders of what might have been her own life. She had to listen to the man she had loved in the pulpit and see another woman sitting in the pew she had hoped to occupy.

St Harmon was a parish without a real vicarage, and though so different with its mountains, streams and rugged moorland, yet having in its loneliness a similarity to Croft. Possibly Katharine was unnerved. But the Bredwardine living was offered to Kilvert, so potentially to her as well. That would have meant a house of immense charm set in a superb position, with a social life in Monnington, Moccas and Staunton all at hand and with large and hospitable houses. All this, as well as Kilvert, she rejected. Instead she left home and trained to be a nurse. We know of the broken engagement, for Charlotte Heanley compiled a pamphlet on the records of the family. A copy of this was lent to Eva Farmery who was researching Katharine Heanley. Charlotte had previously sent this copy to her sister Dr K. Heanley who by then had read Kilvert's diary. She penned in by the date of Katharine's death in 1891; "This is the Kathleen of the Rev. Kilvert's diary. He was engaged to her, but she broke it off".

While Katharine was away training, her mother suffered a stroke. Even then, with all the moral pressures of the time, she refused to come home to nurse her mother. She was inflexible of purpose, and it was her cousin Charlotte who undertook the duties of nursing the sick woman and running the home. In 1883 she had to return, for her father was struck down by a seizure while talking with his foreman in the yard. He was transformed from a bustling, vigorous and forceful man to an unhappy invalid. They left the Grange and

127

moved to Burgh-le-Marsh and there, in July 1884, he hanged himself from the bed-post. A verdict of temporary insanity was returned at the inquest. Two years later, in February 1886, Katharine was offered the post of Matron at Boston Cottage Hospital. She accepted the position with the proviso that her mother could accompany her paying her own expenses of one guinea a week.

There, Katherine proved, as one might have expected, a most capable matron. She had the entire charge of the hospital, not only of the nursing staff, but also the management. All went well until 1890 when she underwent a serious operation. Its nature has not been specified. She made an apparently good recovery, and went back to her post, but in the spring of 1891 she fell ill with influenza, and experienced the all too common post-influenzal depression.

Katharine died suddenly one early morning the following September. At the inquest it was revealed that she had been depressed on the very night a nurse had seen her go to her room. The night-nurse, Rachel Mary Self, had heard movement in the room, immediately above her own, at ten to five in the morning. She then heard the sound of a key turning in the lock, followed by heavy breathing which alarmed her. The porter was called and the door forced. They found Katharine dead, face downward, and the key broken in the lock.

A Dr Pilchard gave evidence. He knew her well; he knew of her extensive knowledge of narcotics. He was aware that she was in the habit of taking them to relieve intolerable pain. The report of the post-mortem revealed an unhealthy condition in her heart, and some diseased tissues in the brain, which could account for her depression. Death was considered by the doctor to be due to syncope, a failure in the operation of the heart. But there was another piece of evidence, fixed to the pin cusion on her dressing table. It was a classic note. It read: "My own crass stupidity is to blame. I cannot meet life's duties".

The coroner in summing up stressed the painful character of the case. He underlined Katharine's great respectability and manifold talents. He reminded the jury of the honourable position her father and family held in the County of Lincoln. If she had taken a narcotic, he hazarded, she would have been profoundly insensible. He stressed the degeneration of her heart and expatiated on his not infrequent experience of people having left papers which misled, implying suicide where in fact the death was due to natural causes. The jury, so powerfully guided, returned a verdict of syncope.

In his diary Kilvert once wrote: "'De Mortuis nil nisi bonum': speak only good of the dead". One is not even tempted to judge Katharine, for one is moved to pity. A thought hovers, but it is like the marsh mists, insubstantial: did she blame herself for Kilvert's death? She was a woman burdened with unattainable ideals, she was obsessive. But Kilvert had died twelve years before. All we can say is that few lovers were so ill-starred as Katharine Heanley and Frank Kilvert when they met at the charming wedding in the serene church of Findon that glorious August day.

# 17.

# St Harmon

The parish of Monnington-on-Wye was offered to and accepted by William Smith in 1875. Until then he and his wife Thersie had lived in Bath at Sydney College. The change for Smith was great indeed, for he left a busy city for an extremely quiet parish in a very rural area. He was a little surprised at the rusticity of some of his fellow clergy at Deanery meetings, but he soon adapted. He was fond of country life, he was a keen shot with a rifle and a good fisherman. Thersie, Kilvert's older sister, found herself back in the vicarage environment in which she had been brought up.

They lived in the large brick built vicarage, with big windows and a rambling garden with paddocks and orchards that ended in one of the glories of Monnington, the mile long Walk of Scots Pines planted at the end of the seventeenth century to commemorate the restoration of the Monarchy. There are other delights in minute Monnington. One is the church built in 1679 with the fittings, bench pews, screen, royal court of arms and altar rails all of the same date. It is remarkable that the barley sugar columns all escaped renovation at the beginning of the nineteenth century. Certainly Kilvert does not remark upon it. It was too simple and classical a building for him to love; his eyes, no doubt, found it stark, lacking in gothic features and wanting in prettiness. He reserves his interest for the lychgate and the nameless stone by the tower, then thought to be Glendower's tomb. It is, in fact, much older.

Monnington was a place which was important to him, first for Thersie's sake and her daughter Florence. Then it was the place where he received fateful letters, one the farewell of Ettie, the other the letter sounding out whether he would be interested in the parish of St Harmon. On the afternoon of April 20th 1876, after receiving

130

Ettie's farewell, as he walked to Bredwardine through the pines which sighed like the sound of the sea, his spirits rose. Just like today the walk seems flat land, rising slowly to Brobury Scar, and then suddenly through the trees the river is seen, many feet below. It is a surprising and beautiful view, and is indeed another of Monnington's delights. Kilvert wrote:

> Especially as I saw it this afternoon, the lovely valley gleaming bright in the clear shining after rain, the thickly wooded hillsides veiled with tender blue delicate mists through which the brilliant evening sun struck out jewels of gold where he lit upon the upland slopes and hill meadows, while the poplar spires shot up like green and gold flames against the background of brown and purple woods and the river blazed below the grey bridge with a sparkle as of a million diamonds.

That afternoon was almost a prophecy of what was to be. He called on Miss Newton, an old acquaintance of Clyro days, and he went up to the rectory, that specially warm but sedate house by the Wye — the Wye which continues to curve and retreat so shyly.

Four days later came Richard Lister Venables' letter sounding him about St Harmon. He grasps the opportunity, but naturally asks for time to view the place. The statement of this good fortune in the diary is bald and flat. He ponders on the stipend worth between £300 and £400 when the lease of two old pensioned former vicars die. But he refers to his sadness at leaving Langley. The lease refers to the untidy and unfair system, prevailing until the 1940s, of raising pensions for retired clergy. It was an agreed amount deducted from the income of the serving incumbent until the former vicar died. It was not only unfair, it caused unnecessary strain and tension. It meant that a vicar with a young family sometimes was almost forced to long for his predecessor's death.

It is a joyless entry, there is no eager anticipation. He was still unhappy about Ettie and unsure about Katharine. It would seem that this offer of preferment came a fortnight too late. There was no possibility of sharing his fortune with Ettie. It was too late, too late. But was it really? If he had really loved Ettie, could he not have re-opened the relationship? Or did he accept her disappearance from his life as a divine decision that Katharine must be his bride? It reveals the old passivity in Kilvert, something even a little mystical.

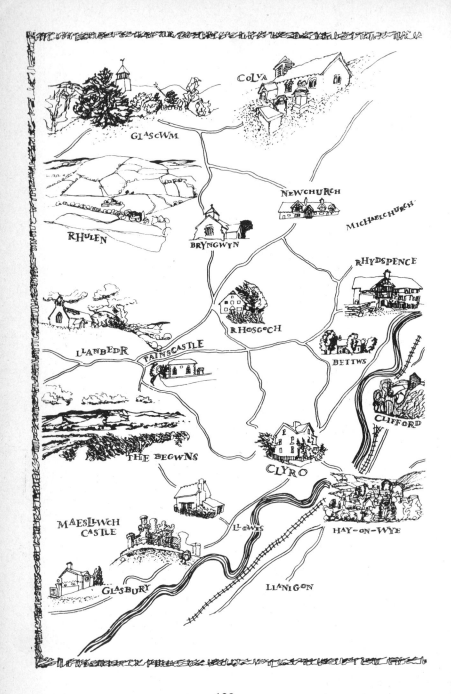

COLVA

GLASCWM

NEWCHURCH

MICHAELCHURCH

RHULEN

BRYNGWYN

RHYDSPENCE

RHOSGOCH

LLANBEDR

PAINSCASTLE

BETTWS

CLIFFORD

THE BEGWNS

CLYRO

MAESLLWCH CASTLE

LLOWES

HAY-ON-WYE

GLASBURY

LLANIGON

132

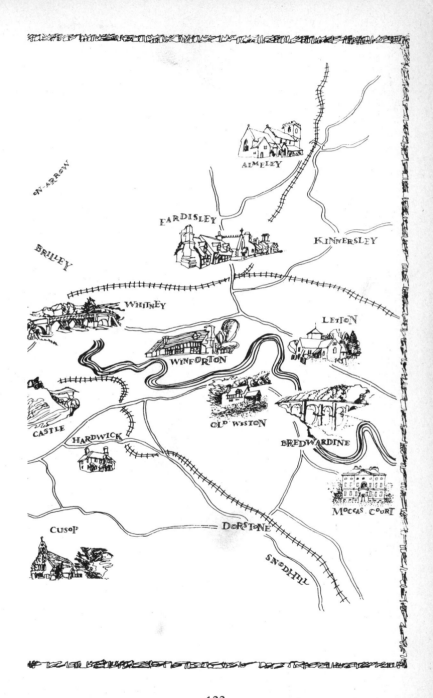

The man who could write, "I fear those grey old men of Moccas", the gnarled and stunted oak trees, and turn the sun into a god when writing, must also have had a very strong sense of the divinity of God. With hindsight it is easy for us to say to him: 'Go, declare your love, secure your bride, be bold in all matters of love and war'.

The days that follow have no mention of St Harmon. Kilvert was revisiting Clyro, seeing the old places and old friends, and going into raptures over the dreamy beauty of yet another love, Florence Hill with her soft golden hair. Florence played the piano:

> Her head was slightly turned on one side as she played and there came over her lovely face a rapt far-away look, self-forgetful, self-unconscious, a look as of one divinely inspired. She seemed to me to be the daughter of the Bards. So pure, so heavenly, so perfect in her beauty.

He did not marry Florence Hill;, no one did. Her latter days were spent in quiet gentility in Llandrindod Wells. But to the end she kept her other-wordly charm and gentleness and to the end of her life that soft hair forever slipped from its bun. So Kilvert had delights enough to write of without reaching out to an unknown future. There is the possibility also that Katharine was mentioned with St Harmon and the scissors snipped all references out. Or maybe, William Plomer thought St Harmon so shadowy a part of Kilvert's career that he would erase as many references as possible.

Kilvert's first encounter with St Harmon came when he stayed at Llysdinam with the Venables in May 1876. Quite certainly the two men would discuss the pros and cons. Mr Venables would take the realistic line that as long as Kilvert remained in Langley he would only be his father's curate and that it was by no means certain the diocese would let Kilvert follow him as incumbent, particularly as Squire Ashe might spike the wheels. At dinner that night de Winton, the Archdeacon of Brecon, arrived. This must have been a preconcerted action, for the Venables were intent on finding Kilvert a living, and they wished the Archdeacon to know their protegé better.

Next day Kilvert and the Archdeacon had breakfast together. Both then went their own way, Kilvert going to St Harmon by train. He was able to reach the inaccessible upland parish more easily than anyone could today. The train stopped close by the church. His first impression was of the "handsome, pleasant-faced woman, very stout, who lives in a cottage on the line". She was the station master. The church clerk's son leaning idly on the gate offered to get the church key. He was a dentist's apprentice on sick leave from London. Together they entered the church yard:

> The church was built in the Dark Ages of fifty years ago and was simply hideous. But ugly as it appeared externally the interior was worse and my heart sank within me like a stone as I entered the door. A bare, cold squalid interior and high ugly square boxes for seats, three-decker pulpit and desk, no stone, a flimsy alter rail, a ragged faded altar cloth, a singing gallery with a broken organ, a dark little box for a vestry and a roof in bad repair, admitting the rain. Such was St Harmon's church as I first saw it.

It was displaying all the neglect that he had managed to eradicate from Langley Burrell Church. Langley Burrell was, though, a building of great beauty, whereas this was one of the boxes, much like the non-conformist chapels that he so disliked.

The clerk's son played Martin Luther's hymn on the broken winded organ whilst Kilvert pumped the wheezing bellows. Later as they left, the young man pointed out to Kilvert the grave of Frederick Joseph Foxton, who was known as 'the Atheist of Bwlch Gwynne'. Foxton is an odd faint figure who lurks rather than thrives in literary history. He was a theologian who lost his faith and renounced his orders. He built himself a very small house, Bwlch Gwynne Isaf, in a narrow pass where the river Wye, in good weather a mere stream strewn with boulders, meets the Marteg coming down from St Harmon. He abandoned this house and built one much larger and more spacious some yards higher up the valley, still with the river bounding the garden. Kilvert knew of him and in March 1870, on his way to the opening of an iron church at Hysfa Common, mentions both the first house and the later pretty Glyn Gwyn. Foxton was at that moment living there. He died in December 1870.

Kilvert revelled in literary connections and it is fascinating to conjecture what memories of Thomas Carlyle he might have conjured from 'the Atheist'. We might have had another view of the battlefield tour in Germany that Carlyle and Foxton made. Foxton had recalled sitting at the doors of their inn in the sunshine "under curls of wreathing tobacco smoke". He liked watching Carlyle on trains listening and watching his fellow passengers with his "grim bearded Saracenic visage".

Carlyle in 1851 described Foxton as "not a genial man but he is healthy and practical; reminds you of an Englishman who has found out that his loom won't go. A wonderful good humour considering his situation, Ci-Devant". But it was after the tour in the footsteps of Frederick the Great that relations frayed a little. For on long journeys Carlyle found him neither particularly companionable nor helpful, "but dull, blustering and vigorously incompetent". We have to remember that Carlyle was a neurotic traveller, fearful that he might not sleep well, always nervous about accommodation and trains, and always carrying with him his "grumbling indigestion". In fact as Foxton became exhausted so Carlyle gained in energy. As one wilted the other throve.

Leaving the churchyard Kilvert went to the school where he met twenty-two children and their "soured, disappointed and complaining" schoolmaster. But just as Kilvert was thinking him a difficult man to have in his parish, he learnt that he was leaving and taking a school in Northamptonshire.

At Temple Bar Kilvert was kindly received by a jolly woman, wife of the church clerk, who gave him cakes and ale and his spirits revived. A boy and girl returned from school for dinner and he kissed the pretty child which made her brother laugh. The good humoured mother called out "I hope you will come here and be our Vicar". The day had become glorious and he walked the four and a half miles down the rough track to Aber Marteg. He went up the Llangurig road and looked down the steep bank into the chimney pots of 'Bwlch Gwynne Isaf' (the vicarage) which was let to a tenant, and also at Foxton's home 'Glyn Grog'.

He then walked the fourteen miles back to Llysdinam, thinking very hard of the pros and the cons of such a parish. He thought of the church and what must be done. He remembered the people he had encountered and above all he recalled that 'I was entirely alone except for the presence of the mountain sheep'. It was the landscape he loved and felt free in.

Back at Llysdinam he found old friends had arrived, Tomkyns and Fanny Dew. They must all have talked of his prospects and said how pleasant it would be to have him fairly nearby once more.

It was slowly becoming more attractive to him, so that when he awoke next morning he rose, had breakfast, left a note to say where he was going and set off to see the upper part of St Harmon. This shows how relaxed and easy his relationship with the Venables was; indeed, he was virtually 'a son of the house'.

He went beyond St Harmon on the train and alighted at Tylwch amongst the mountains. At a watershed he found all the streams running the other way to join the Severn, not the Wye. He was touched when the one-armed station master told him that peace between the English and the Welsh had been signed there in the reign of Edward I, and that Tylwch meant 'house of peace'. Following the river and leaping streams, he found himself now in Radnor, now in Montgomeryshire. He thought of a girl he had known from these hills, Mary Evans, but the woman in a plaid shawl whom he asked did not recollect her. He then set off for Llanidloes nine miles away, falling in with a tall handsome young farmer and his dog who had "all the beautiful and native Welsh courtesy". He was sorry when their ways were parted and he walked down and down into "Llanidloes, beautiful Llanidloes", and the valley of the Severn "deeply sequestered, embosomed by the mountains on every side and lapped so lovingly amongst the fair blue hills."

One knows that Kilvert's acceptance is no longer in doubt, for the man who longed to find Welsh blood in his veins was enchanted. The kinship, not of blood but of temperament, made him at one with the people and the lovely lonely land. He rushed round the little town with only a quarter of an hour to spare before his train left the long, noble and dignified station, which is still there but now without a railway track. Later it was to have fame, for it carried the first refrigerated compartment in Britain, carrying Plynlimmon mutton to Buckingham Palace for King Edward VII and Queen Alexandra.

When he arrived back Mr Venables cried out, "Well, you are an adventurous young man!" Even allowing for the Venables paternalism it is an indication of the youthfulness of the thirty-six year old Kilvert. It is, possibly, a pointer to a certain immaturity which was at once his charm and his undoing in his career. The institution of Kilvert to the Parish of St Harmon in 1876 was a noted occasion. It is easy to believe that Price Jones the parish clerk was impressed, for all Kilvert's clerical and county friends converged, many in their own carriages, and St Harmon saw more people than it had seen for a long while.

Then comes the break. The notebooks of the period have vanished, almost certainly destroyed by Kilvert's widow — and understandably, as we shall see. It is possible to piece together a little of his life there from a return he made on 26th April 1878 to take the wedding service of David Powell and Maggie Jones. After the service he went to the Sun Inn with the party and then joined them at the farm where he carved. The clerk sitting by him sighed deeply and said, "Tis a pity but what you had stayed here". These are the kind things parishioners always say to former vicars, pleasing to hear but not always to be taken too seriously.

It is certain he carried out his duties with his usual vigour. He tidied the church, he gave at his own expense new prayer books and within that country seeing the sturdy independent people who populated it, one may be sure he walked many happy miles visiting. In fact when Hastings Smith, Thersie's eldest son, went to St Harmon in later years to see the place and forlornly hoped to find the missing diary, he met in Rhayader

a wizened looking old fellow, yellow faced with a bunch of gray whiskers, he turned eyes on me, which were keen and intelligent. Yes, I should have taken him for a shoe-maker, or cobbler. When I told him who I was, and of my enquiries he was at once interested. 'Yes I do mind *Mr Kilbert* Mind him I do well. I was a young lad those days and worked with the horses. In the stable yard at The Crown I worked, till I took up my father's trade. Yes, I mind Mr Kilbert. He lived at the 'Old Bank House' just across the street. They pulled it down a year or two ago and built a new 'un.' And in truth it was a very new Bank House which stood there now. New red brick and shining brass plates. 'Mr Kilbert never lived at St Harmon's', he continued. 'Lived in Rhayader he did, and went up to his parish by train on week days. Sundays he walked up or was druv. Most always he walked. Bad weather or snowy roads. I have druv Mr Kilbert myself to St Harmon's of a Sunday. And I mind driving a young lady up with him. No, he wasn't a married gentleman. Ah! A real nice gentleman was Mr Kilbert' enthused the old cobbler, using a *b* instead of a *v*. 'Quiet gentleman, great black beard. Like a foreign gentleman, as my father used to say. No, we don't see such gentleman nowadays.

Nor such beards. 'E was a great walker, sir. Many a pair of boots
my father soled for Mr Kilbert. And fancy you his nephew.

There are echoes of Kilvert's guide in Dolgelly, whose compliment
"You're a splendid walker, Sir" had earned him a brandy and
water. This time the story earned the teller a pint of beer.

One sees in this record the same literary quality which all the
Kilverts seemed to share. Hastings though shared other
characteristics of his uncle. He had the same tact and openness that
charmed. On his wanderings he encountered an old lady who was
so enchanted by him that she gave him a small glass cream jug
which her mother had used when pouring out the Vicar's tea.
Indeed it is not too fanciful to see in the photographs of the
Edwardian straw-hatted and moustached man with dark eyebrows
and bright eyes and a clear shadow where a thick beard could be the
likeness of his uncle; and a lingering of the sallow Squire Coleman,
Kilvert's grandfather.

But who was the young lady who was driven up to St Harmon?
Thoughts of marriage to Katharine were looming large in Kilvert's
mind and plans. Was it Katharine who was with him in the
carriage? Some have thought so, but I inclined to agree with
William Price that it was unlikely as there was no chaperone. We
therefore considered it to be one of his sisters, Dora or Fanny. Yet
the determined chin of Katharine still intrudes. Katharine was a
strong minded young woman, and if she had seen fit to inspect St
Harmon, her future home, nothing would have stopped her.
Whichever woman did come, she saw the remoteness of the place
and the unsuitability of Bwlch Gwynne as a vicarage, too far
removed from the church and far too small.

Did the objections of Katharine to St Harmon result in a search
for another living? And did those ever useful and influential friends
at Llysdinam help? We shall probably never know. What we do
know is that suddenly, when away from the parish, the Rev John
Houseman, incumbent of Bredwardine, died in September 1877.
The patron of the living was Miss Newton, daughter of a former
incumbent. She lived in The Cottage, a Victorian villa in
Bredwardine. Her father had bought the advowson of the parish;
that is, the right to choose and present a priest to the living.

One wonders if William and Thersie Smith may have had a hand

139

at this point in Kilvert's career. The present writer thinks it was the character of Kilvert alone that prompted Miss Newton, for she remembered his visit when he had walked over from Monnington. He had listened and admired the organ she had just installed in her house. Kilvert was at long last being accepted not just as a pleasant amiable fellow but as a person in his own right.

So in his Rhayader lodgings he received the invitation and this unquestioning generous and simple soul would give thanks to the providence of a beneficient God. He would, at last, be able to enter into a parish, a house of his very own with a wife upon his arm. Without doubt he dreamt of the children he longed for. Light was breaking in upon the career of Francis Kilvert, and a new dawn was there.

And yet at that moment Katharine decided upon another break, the break of the engagement. This is deeply hurtful to any man, but to Kilvert deeper than most, for he never had been able to do anything but accept a rebuff. It had its own irony too, which almost makes him a creation of Thomas Hardy, just as Katharine is one of George Gissing's. It was a far more cruel irony than that which Kilvert used, so often in his gentle humour. He was a devastated man.

# 18.

# Bredwardine

The last house Kilvert lived in was the vicarage of Bredwardine. It is set on the banks of the Wye just inside the boundary of the county and diocese of Hereford. He had thought to come to this calm and bewitching place either a married man, or one about to be, but things were going wrong. 'Jilt' would be too cruel a word for either character in this unhappy drama. Kilvert took up his parish and his home under severe disappointment. Allied with this was the fact that he was now in his mid-thirties, and some of the fire of youth — and he kept his longer than most — was dying. But ownership of a parson's freehold gave him a definite confidence; that confidence the house still holds today.

Of all Kilvert's houses this has the finest position. It is larger than his birthplace, probably equal in size to the vicarage of Langley Burrell and considerably larger that Mr Venables' vicarage in Clyro. This is a unique house wearing nobility with an easy grace, and with a garden, like a train, sweeping down to the river. It is stuccoed and has most pacific battlements, not square-edged, but like small rounded Dutch gables. Inside, the lofty rooms must have delighted the tall man, giving him an added sense of space. It is a place to be proud of.

There is another quality, even more important. It is a place of an almost eerie peace. Three very different people, the owner, the present incumbent of the combined parishes and the present writer, each with only their insticts and susceptibilities to guide them, think this is an especial peace. One is tempted to think this atmosphere was left by Kilvert, but it is older; far, far older. Is it a trick of the landscape making a spot in a quiet area still quieter, or is it of another dimension, another level of consciousness which is quietly alerted? One is saddened that Kilvert enjoyed this house for so short a time. But we remember that houses are but houses, they only seem durable. Kilvert left something more precious behind, his diary. This is the living word, the only real defiant demolisher of time and death.

On St Andrew's Day (patron saint of the Church) 30th November 1877, Kilvert was instituted to the living of Bredwardine in the county and Diocese of Hereford. It is a scattered parish with fields and woods and hills dividing small gatherings of dwellings. The feature of main importance is the brick bridge with its six arches and triangular places at the side of the causeway where the pedestrian can stand to let the traffic flow by. It was built in 1759, joining the two parishes of Bredwardine and Brobury on the Hereford side. The river at this point is particularly beautiful, enclosed by steep wooded banks and the current running in sudden deeps and shallows with rapids above the bridge.

The parish Kilvert tended was more populated in his time. It was large partly because in 1793 George Jarvis, a rich leather merchant, left the sum of £30,000 in a trust for the poor of Bredwardine, Staunton on Wye and Letton. Many shrewd families, some feckless, saw the advantage of living in a parish where a small 'welfare state' prevailed. This caused some problems for the Trustees and Kilvert was one of them.

Once there had been a castle in the parish close to the church. The church is full of interest to the historian, the architect and those who like romantic sites. Its grey stones rise up from a mound where an ancient yew tree grows. The porch on the south side covers the Norman doorway with its tufa stonework which is no doubt local from Moccas. Inside, the church has a most curious lean to the north. The nave, chancel and sanctuary all turn in that direction. A lean to the left of the chancel is not uncommon, but here the entire church is askew. By the altar are two recumbent effigies. One, greatly damaged in the past, is of a gigantic Knight, Walter Baskerville, who died in 1369. The other, in a much better state of preservation, is Sir Roger Vaughan who was killed as he defended Henry V at Agincourt, in 1415: such patriotic links with history would not have been lost on Kilvert. The whole setting is romantic, charming and rustic. It is like an early Victorian engraving for a book of verse, in stone, grass and living wood.

Behind the church is the vicarage, stuccoed with very fine and fluid carved battlements, and large French windows looking down terraces to the river. Few houses have a finer position. But characteristically Kilvert never mentions the interior. We look almost in vain for descriptions of rooms in the diary, and when they do occur they are usually of cottage or farm kitchens. The front door of the vicarage leads into a hall pillared on one side; it was there that Kilvert met his parishioners and where tithes were paid. The hall leads to a wide corridor containing the staircase and doors to the three main rooms; the dining room, the study and the impressive drawing room. This room contains two fine and vast panelled doors of oak which can be opened into the study. It is a house of which the possessor can justifiably be proud.

The church and the vicarage standing side by side make a reality of the idealized image many have of the country parson's setting. The diary we have of life within these walls begins on 31st December 1877 and closes on 13th March 1879. It amounts to only one hundred and fourteen pages of print. There was more, much more, which William Plomer never saw and which Hastings Smith never set eyes upon. Those are the pages that Kilvert's widow removed. They would have told us a great deal.

Although Kilvert had been overwhelmed at Katharine's decision, still one is aware of a new confidence in the inner man. It is easy to imagine that all this began with his entry into Bredwardine, but it may well have begun in St Harmon. Hitherto he had been a curate, a very good curate to Richard Lister Venables and then to his own father, taking on much more responsibility in a trying situation. He was however the curate, a special kind of servant, sharing the same rank as his employer, yet still not the parson, which only the incumbent can be. Parson is a word derived from the Latin 'persona', a marked person. The Anglican clergyman, less now than then, had an area which was spiritually his own. His responsibility was to God, then his bishop, for the people within that parish. He feels that he has a special status, partly divine and partly social, but with a quality of apartness. These feelings have become blurred and parishes have lost much of their individuality by being — and necessarily so — amalgamated. The clergyman no longer belongs to a distinct area, he roves over much larger tracts and a far greater proportion of his flock are almost totally indifferent to his role and the church's too. This was far from so in 1877, when the Church of England was at its zenith. As A.L.le Quesne says pertinently, "Kilvert was a country parson at the peak of the agricultural boom". The depression in the countryside came at the end of the century. Farmers went bankrupt, including Katharine Heanley's family. The drift to the towns came back again.

In Kilvert's time modernisation was in its infancy, and only in the latter portion do we hear of steam-engines in the fields. In his day, the land still needed many hands to work it. It was into this settled, ordered rural community that Kilvert came with an intimate knowledge gained from a life-span. He settled in easily and immediately, he knew his role and identified with it. He was fortunate too that unlike his father he had no tyrannical squire to contend with.

There was humour as well as satisfaction when he wrote in the third paragraph of the entry for the last day of 1877, "I called on my tenant at the Rectory Farm, Brobury". The next day, up at Crafta Webb, he visited the tailor and shoemaker, "my tenants". "The shoemaker took me round the little meadows which he holds of me" and still with a sense of ownership he continued: "I met James Davies, my churchwarden". He was greeted with great courtesy, often deference.

Even as recently as twenty-five years ago a country parson knew his fields, his barns and above all his tenants, but gradually the bureaucracy of the dioceses eroded responsibility for them from the incumbent. Many clergy wished it so. But with its disappearance the incumbent's particular interest in the working of the parish and being a part of that system vanished.

That same New Year's Day 1878, his parents came to visit him and his sister Dora, who was already keeping house for him. As was usual in clerical households in those days a visit was also a working holiday. After accidents with the carriage and inevitable delays the old man drank a quick cup of tea, and was hurried to the church where he preached at a special evening service. It was not until the next day that Kilvert was able to show his parents the territory of his not inconsiderable domain. His father found it all much larger and more beautiful than he had imagined and was happy for his son.

All this helped to add to Kilvert's inner confidence, and it is not fanciful to see that he carries it with him when he returns to

Langley alone, leaving his father in charge at Bredwardine. He consults Mrs Ashe about the connections of the family with Moccas Court, the great estate adjacent to Bredwardine and the home of Lord George Cornewall. There seems a lack of tension in the sentence: "I went into Langley House and sat an hour talking".

Back in Bredwardine three weeks later there was a web of local commitments, the school, the Wyeside Clerical Association, and the Tithe dinner:

> About 50 tithe payers came, most of them very small holders, some paying as little as 9d. As soon as they had paid their tithe to Mr Haywood in the front hall they retired into the back hall and regaled themselves with bread, cheese and beer, some of them eating and drinking the value of the tithe they had paid. The tithe-paying began about 3 p.m. and the stream went on until six. At 7 I sat down to dinner with the farmers. Haywood took the foot of the table. His son sat on my left and Price of Bedcote on my right hand. The other guests were Griffiths of the Pentre, James Davies of Fine St, George Davies of Benfield and young Thomas Davies of the Old House, Edmund Preece, young Parry of Dolfac and Mr Bates the schoolmaster.
>
> 'The Pen Pistyll turkey' [a present from St Harmon] boiled looked very noble when it came to table. George Davies of Benfield was so impressed with the size of the bird that he declared it must be a 'three year old' and he did not hear the last of this all the evening. At the foot of the table there was roast beef, and at the sides jugged hare and beefsteak pie, preceded by pea soup, and in due course followed by plum pudding, apple tart, mince pies and blancmange, cheese and desert. It was a very nice dinner, thanks to Dora, and I think they all liked it and enjoyed themselves. After dinner Mr Haywood proposed my health very kindly and I made a little speech. We broke up at 10.30. Thersie came over to help us and spent the night here.

There is a serenity, the old content is rising in him again, and it is enshrined in one entry written on 24th February of 1878:

> After luncheon I sat in the warm sheltered nook by the greenhouse looking down the river watching the lights changing, broadening, narrowing, vanishing on the soft dark stream. The sky was grey and silvery, very soft, pleasant and delicate, and the sun shone out warm by whiles. The willows were reddening with

buds by the water courses. From the lower garden came the
rushing of a little brook or spring running into the river. Now and
then a heavy fish jumped with a loud splash in the deep water off
the garden, the birds were singing softly, the cooing of
woodpigeons came gently from the cedars and the river orchard,
and the plaintive cry of the moorhens rose from the waterside.
Then at 2 o'clock the 4 sweet bells rung an hour before service and
from the Church came faint and sweet the roll of the organ.

The parish in which he now found himself was older and more
established than either Clyro or St Harmon. The church, the
vicarage and the school were all markedly superior, and in many
respects superior to Langley Burrell as well.

Kilvert's love of teaching re-asserted itself and he taught once
more in the singularly charming stone built school lying long and
low very sympathetically in its wooded dingle behind the Red Lion
Inn. He had a happy relationship with Mr Bates the headmaster, in
spite of the episode when Algy Bates seemingly put some swan shot
through Miss Catherine Newton's bedroom window. One senses
that Miss Newton was somewhat officious and wished to be the
Lady of the Manor. The headmaster, without doubt, received
complaints from her about the behaviour of the children and she
was not loved by the younger generation. Kilvert kept his peace all
round.

But now another factor begins to emerge. In spite of the idyllic
setting of the vicarage and parish Kilvert frequently was unwell.
Until then his disabilities had been confined to his eyes. Some think
that he had a squint. If that is so, and it is not unlikely, it would
account for his attacks of neuralgia and headaches. They could
easily stem from strain in trying to overcome the deficiency in his
vision. It could also be shortsightedness, for he mentions early in
the diary "blundering near a beehive in my blind way". In the 1870
trip to Cornwall he was unable to see a seal quite close at hand
which Hockin pointed out to him. In Clyro he suffered a very bad
boil and the Venables made him lie on a sofa in the garden. The
medical view is that boils are usually signs of lowered resistance and
a lack of fresh fruit.

In March he had a bad headache and a cold and great tightness in
his chest. Lady Cornewall brought him a bottle of Syrup of
Hypophosphate of Lime — whether it worsened or improved his

condition we do not know! He continued his duties but had a persistent cough. It did not prevent him going to Rhayader but the high altitude and keen air made him worse. He had a bout of neuralgia, and must have looked ill for his friends and acquaintances were concerned. His cough frightened them, for a cough to a Victorian spelled one thing: tuberculosis.

He returned home to Langley so that his mother could look after him. Dr Spencer examined him and pronounced congestion of the lungs. It seems very likely that he had viral pneumonia, a slow relentless illness which requires the very thing Kilvert denied himself: rest. It always leaves the patient depressed and the entry he made on 9th March on the terrace of his old home is typical of post infection depression:

> After how many illnesses such as this have I taken my first convalescent walk on the sunny terrace and always at this time of year when the honeysuckle leaves were shooting green and the apricot blossoms were dawning and the daffodils in blow. But some day will come the last illness from which there will be no convalescence and after which there will be no going out to enjoy the sweet sights and sounds of the earthly spring, the singing of the birds, the opening of the fruit blossoms, the budding dawn of green leaves, and the blowing of the March daffodils. May I then be prepared to enter into the everlasting Spring and to walk among the birds and flowers of Paradise.

It was a house of sickness. His mother fell ill with rheumatic gout. Whilst she was still ill he returned to Bredwardine and ran into a blinding snowstorm on his way home. There was a persistent east wind and even Dora fainted at family prayers. His cough persisted. When at its worst the vicar of Eardisley visited him, he must have been frightened at Kilvert's condition, and he set about seeking another place for him. As a result, when Kilvert went to the Palmer garden party at Eardisley vicarage, his host took him aside and offered him from Canon Walsham How, the great hymn-writer, the permanent chaplaincy at Cannes in the south of France. He added that it might improve Kilvert's health.

Naturally this unexpected proposition threw him into some consternation. He wrote letters seeking advice from the Venables, an unknown friend, Canon Walsham How, and his father. He went over to Moccas Court to talk to Miss Cornewall who had just returned from the south of France. Three days later he was still thinking about it and writing letters.

His health cannot have been so poor, and his lungs must have been in good order, for he walked up Bredwardine Hill to Arthur's Stone, a considerable climb. Possibly when walking there, calling at cottages and receiving a friendly welcome, he decided that the aridities of an English community in exile, all of one class, was not for him. His decision was wise, for he was *in excelsis* an English country parson. Though he died only a little over a year later, his death had nothing to do with either his neuralgia or his lungs.

There was still though a pre-occupation with death and illness. He notes the anniversary of his predecessor's death. But we have to remember that death was a constant companion of the Victorians; it was pervasively present. In November Kilvert was low once more, this time with haemorrhoids which he in good Old Testament terms refers to as "emerods" such as afflicted the Philistines at Ashdod. Dr Giles came over from Staunton to attend him.

There was something troubling Kilvert, and he does not record it in his diary. On 24th November 1878 whilst asleep on the sofa in his study he had a dream in which he seemed to be fighting for his life with some dreadful Power. When it discovered it was unable to kill him it flung him on the sofa and departed in a rage. In the struggle he had feared that the lamp would topple over. He seems to have been in a state of anxiety. It could have been his health, his debts (he had spent a lot on furnishing the house), or anger with Katharine and his abiding need for a wife for real fulfilment. It seemed he would never be truly fulfilled until he had children of his own. Yet, next day, he went up to Rhayader with the country under snow and ice and he took no hurt at first. It seems that his moods were unstable, for then he had another sore throat and was suffering from a severe head cold. He recovered and visited many parishioners. Christmas was drawing close.

On Christmas Eve, he was told that a son of David and Margaret Davies of Old Weston, where the father was a shepherd, had died. Kilvert walked up to see them, and met the father on his way to order a coffin. The man was both grieving and angry. Kilvert discovered that it was the younger son, Davie, who had died. At the cottage Margaret Davies was glad to see him and took him up to the bedroom: "I never saw death look so beautiful". He was deeply moved and he bent to kiss the white forehead which felt marmoreal to his touch. The distressed mother told him of the illness and the unearthly, beautiful and comforting visions the boy had had as he lay dying. He saw children dancing in a garden; there was music and wonderful birds, and more oddly the men of Weston, his father's contemporaries.

On Christmas Day the funeral took place. Great clouds of snow blinded the mourners. The men of Weston carried the small coffin and they had a cold coming of it, but they were only twenty minutes late. The father wept openly and bitterly and in the snow a woman held an umbrella over Kilvert's head as he made the committal. When the service was over Kilvert tried to make the mourning party come into the vicarage and warm themselves, but they would not. They were too stunned and grieved to think. They went into the church and awaited the evening service. It became darker and darker, and Kilvert had to move to the window in order to see the print of the Bible. He preached on the text 'There was no room for them in the inn'. With tact but with some sentiment he linked the new grave in Bredwardine with the manger in Bethlehem.

The rest of his day was busy, with another service at Brobury and an evening with Dora at Miss Newton's. All the while though the death and the funeral was in his mind and during the following days he wrote his poem 'In loving memory of Little Davie', which was published in the *Hereford Times* of 7th February 1879.

I can add something further to this story. In my own researches, perhaps the most tangible but also frustrating link I have made with Kilvert was through Mrs Price of Cusop. She is a pretty old lady with a mass of white hair put up in curls on the top of her head in the Edwardian manner. She is now one hundred years old. Sitting by this centenarian I felt that I made strides, decade by decade, into the past. On the wall by her bed was a large fine photograph of Mrs Price as a young girl with her hair unpinned, falling to her shoulders in waving masses. The girl and the old lady were clearly recognisable.

I was talking to the niece of Margaret Davies, little Davie's mother. She of course never knew her cousin Davie, but she knew his parents and his siblings. Margaret Davies continued to live at the Old Weston until her death in the 1940s, dying there. As I talked of Kilvert Mrs Price's voice sharpened just a little and I received a reproof: "We always said 'Mr Kilvert' and my aunt never said anything but 'dear Mr Kilvert'".

Margaret Davies had a devotion to Mr Kilvert for the remainder of her life, and polished brasses in Bredwardine Church until the day came when the candlesticks were brought to her, since she could make the journey no longer. An album of photographs was produced, and most of them dated from the seventies and eighties of the last century. Now came my moment of profound disappointment. A page opened to a series of neatly dressed women in the virtual uniform of young country matrons: black bodice, a touch of lace at the throat, a brooch and hair centrally parted and drawn back into a bun. One sweet grave faced woman had a child on her lap, and the question leapt from me: "Could that be Margaret Davies and little Davie?" The answer came, "I am afraid I cannot see them now. A year ago, I knew them all".

Still hoping, I eased out the carte-de-visite photo, longing, urging for a name, a clue on the back. All I learnt was that the studio was in Carmarthen, which made the link with Bredwardine less likely. But I learnt more of Aunt Margaret, and a time sequence like an unfolding screen opened out before me, as I was told of visits every Bank Holiday to the Old Weston, on bicycles and then in motor-bike and side car and later in a car. It showed the steady climb in this century of wealth more equally spread, and a withdrawal from the class structures of Kilvert's day.

Meanwhile for Kilvert life in Bredwardine continued. Here he enjoyed the first real security of his own, for he was in a nest which did not repose on a "rotten bough". He had, as did indeed his father, the parson's freehold which guaranteed the house for the incumbent's lifetime unless he committed some severe misdemeanour.

Riches however still eluded him, but he did not seem unduly concerned about his debts. He had furnished the vicarage very largely from the well-known and expensive firm of Schoolbreds in London. Back in January 1878 he had received their bill for £230.9.6d, and it was not until May that he was able to send them £50 on account and in July that he was able to pay the full amount. Like so many clerics he had a fine house, he had an establishment and four servants, and he mixed happily with the gentry of the district. But he was not rich. It is noticeable that still he kept no horse or trap. Accepting the precedent of his father he decided to take in pupils, to supplement his income. His first pupil, and as far as we are aware his last, arrived on 10th January 1879. It was Sam Cowper Coles, the son of the Captain Cowper Coles who went down in the ship of his own design. Sam was therefore the nephew of the Rev. and Mrs Venables.

One can only sigh for Sam. It must have been a lonely life for the boy at the vicarage. We have absolutely no reason to think him retarded, just badly taught, and Kilvert found him "very backward and strangely inaccurate". His ignorance continued to puzzle Kilvert. He took Sam visiting with him and the villagers made much of the fair haired, pink complexioned boy.

That winter was very hard and again, as in Clyro, there had been that now famous Christmas Day of 1878, when the cold water in his running bath was frozen. Out on his lawn Kilvert saw the floes of ice left on the banks by the swollen river which now fell. The previous night it had rushed down, "roaring, cracking and thundering against the bridge like the rolling of a hundred wagons".

At the end of January he went to Langley, and shopping in Bath bought two oleographs and a Kidderminster carpet for his house and a "comprehensive pocket knife" for Arthur the handyman and gardener. Arthur had had many broken nights and a lot of trouble keeping up the fires for the "greenhouse and vinery". This is a small reminder of what little empires country houses were, employing so many, even for a bachelor. However, Dora kept house for him. She was always temperamentally in tune with her brother and she fell easily into the role of the mistress of a vicarage. And it is in this light of Dora's role that we now look at the events leading to Kilvert's own eventual marriage.

On 4th June 1878, after Kilvert's illness and depression, Edward his younger brother had married Nellie Pitcairn at St Barnabas Church in Kensington. The entirety of the diary entries concerning this wedding have a continued note of flatness and even of subjugation. Edward, or 'Perch', was to find a joy, indeed an ecstasy, so long denied his elder brother. This wedding re-opened wounds. The day Kilvert journeyed up to London, he "went out early and walked in the lower garden amongst the dewy roses by the river". What were his thoughts? His real thoughts were probably being repressed, even at that moment, by the Wye.

The wedding is described in the same level tones; where they stayed, where they dressed. The adjectives which always tell one so much about the diarist are "merry" for the breakfast and the wedding generally was "pretty and happy". When it was all over Kilvert and his sister Fanny went down to Faversham to stay with his old friend Richard Hilton. After two days there he walked with Mrs Hilton and Fanny across the lawn and the bridge to the train: "I was very sorrowful to go away, but neither of us said much, it was too sad to talk and we were both heavy-hearted". Was it just the parting that caused such despondency amongst them? Or was it Katharine Heanley? Is it possible that she had timed her final word until after Edward's wedding? The post was so efficient those days that it was possible to gauge accurately the arrival of a letter.

Life continued, as it always does after bereavements and disappointments; it assuages the bruises and hurts. The parish and all its people interested him. Then in the following March of 1879, after a visit to Moccas, Dora showed him a letter that she had received that day from James Pitcairn, Nellie's brother. She, too, had a proposal of marriage. "This took me entirely by surprise, but I foresee that she will do so". Kilvert's surmise was correct. He knew that he would feel her loss keenly, and once again he was forced to look to the future which was something he was never able to do with any ease. His instinct was to live, even better rejoice, in the present moment and look back to a distancing past. Whether he cogitated on marriage for himself in his diary we do not know. These would be the pages destroyed by his future widow who firmly erased Katharine Heanley and even more thoroughly all reference to herself.

Kilvert's courage was rising, his health was much better, and coughs and nose bleeds were things of the past. It is highly unlikely that the parish knew anything of the depths of his anguish. He was saved from real despair by his faith. It was in his character, though, never to recover from rebuffs with sanguinity: to find a wife, as now seemed necessary with Dora's impending departure, appeared daunting, with so many false starts and a wounding repulse behind him. He must have thought fathers to be ogres, and even some women must now become suspect in his eyes.

# 19.

# Marriage

Kilvert's choice of bride fell upon Elizabeth Rowland. He had met her in Paris in 1876 on the visit arranged by his friend Mayhew. It has been suggested that the introduction was not all chance. Probably as happened so often in Kilvert's life, his friends were at work on his behalf. On Thursday 13th March, five months before his wedding-day, Kilvert's diary as we have it ends.

Elizabeth was the daughter of a landowner, John Rowland, who lived in a new but fine house a little outside Wootton near Woodstock in Oxfordshire. Rowland had trained to be a doctor at both St. Thomas's Hospital and Guy's Hospital, but threw up his studies and settled in his native county. It is interesting that Elizabeth's mother was connected with the Prattenton family of Worcester and would have known of Aunt Maria Kilvert. It seems that the Rowlands were well thought of in Wootton and most especially Elizabeth. She took it upon herself to care for the poor, and a god-daughter described her as "eminently suited for a Vicar's wife". That we know so little about her is a mist of her own creation. Her determination to cut out all references to herself in the diary suggests a decisiveness of character. Some have called her the wrong wife for Kilvert, an opinion formed on nothing. It is true that if we compare her photograph with that of Ettie Meredith Brown, we see that she lacks the neat sculptured features: compared with Fanny Thomas the sweet poignancy of youth is missing. But beauty, as no less an authority than Shakespeare tells us, lies in the eye of the beholder. There may have been rhapsodies about Elizabeth, in the diary, to equal descriptions of former loves, even the smaller jumps of the heart like Florence Hill, or even Irish Mary, also referred to in the diary elsewhere.

Rhapsodies, however, seem unlikely, not entirely because

Elizabeth could not inspire them but because Kilvert was now different, a more sober and mature man. The question arises: did Elizabeth suppress anything derogatory to herself in the journal? The answer lies in our knowledge of Kilvert. He is always very slow to make an uncharitable remark even when justified, unless very riled. He was not a critical man.

We know little of Elizabeth Rowland, but of one thing we can be sure; Mayhew would hardly have introduced his dear friend to a harridan! So we are reduced to analysing photographs, an unscientific process which gives ample scope to the imagination and to subjectivity. The studio photograph shows a pleasant faced woman; in the light of Kilvert's love of exciting beauty she seems a little plain, but the deep set eyes have an alertness and some humour and her mouth still more. She was most surely kind and thoughtful. Possibly she was the kind of woman who often remains unmarried and her friends and relatives bemoan that men are so blind in not seeing what an excellent wife is being missed.

There is another photograph, the picture of James Pitcairn and Dora, taken at Langley immediately before they left for their own honeymoon a fortnight before Kilvert's marriage. In it Kilvert stands too; upright, full-faced, showing his straight eyebrows and regular features. He bears a close resemblance to the last Tsar, Nicholas II, who was also a handsome man. Because Kilvert does not smile it has been assumed that he was not happy, and even that his illnesses of the previous eighteen months had taken a severe toll of him. In fact, none of the men smile, and the bridegroom looks like a schoolboy being reproved. Some of the women smile, but not all. Photography at that time was still a serious business.

Sitting immediately in front of Kilvert is his fiancee. Her hair is darker than in the studio portrait, and she is somewhat stiff. She was meeting a host of new and curious relatives. She looks to the camera with interest and concentration. Her ruched dress would appear to be expensive, but she lacks the chic of the daughters of Squire Ashe. These girls all wear the brimmed hats of that year which were replacing the bonnets with lappets of lace tied beneath the chin worn by most other ladies. It can safely be said that Elizabeth would never be in the forefront of fashion. I do not expect Kilvert ever described every article of her apparel as he had that of Ettie Meredith Brown.

Apparently in 1948 William Plomer received an undated letter from a parishioner of Bredwardine telling him a little about Elizabeth: "It was a pleasure his wife used to visit us every year till she died and her niece which is living in Eastbourne she always used to take me on her lap and give me some of her tea. I have a photo of Mr and Mrs Kilvert and a book of poems. They are people worth remembering, if there were more of these about the world would be better off". This long letter with its three full stops tells us so much so simply. It describes Elizabeth as the woman who would have so quietly and unassumingly taken her place by Kilvert's side, visiting the cottages. The child on her lap, the sips of tea; it is a Kilvertian picture. Fate, Kilvert, and possibly his friends, scheming for his welfare, had no doubt chosen suitably enough.

Two of Elizabeth's nieces wrote to the Kilvert Society in the 1940s describing her:

> She was tall, and her face has a very kind, genial expression. She was unselfish, and ready to help anyone in trouble. The villagers of Wootton loved her. She had a Bible class of big girls on Sundays and was constantly visiting the sick and poor of the parish.
>
> She was fond of gardening and knew much about flowers. The birds in winter — even the rooks — came on the terrace when she fed them. Dogs knew, instinctively, that she would take them walks!
>
> Her manner was gentle and her voice soft: an excellent thing in a woman.

This niece adds a very sad little note:

> My aunt survived her husband by thirty years, she died at Redlands, Hartfield Road, Eastbourne [where the family moved, when on the death of her father Hollybank passed into the hands of the youngest brother]. She was taken to Bredwardine Churchyard and lies in the new part, as the space she requested to be reserved for her by her husband's grave was unfortunately — and to her grief — allowed to be used for someone else.
>
> As long as her health permitted, she visited Bredwardine at Eastertide, when the beautiful custom of decking graves with primroses was still kept up. I well remember going on the pilgrimage with her on one occasion.

When Dora was away on her honeymoon in Ambleside, she kept a journal. It shows how many of her brother's tastes and prejudices she shared. Both hated tourists, never seeming to realize that they were tourists themselves. She thought of her brother on his wedding day 20th August 1879 and she hoped that the weather was as fine as it was in the Lake Distict. It was not.

Great preparations had been made for the marriage and the villagers had raised arches of evergreen and flowers over the road for the much loved Miss Rowland, who was so familiar a figure in Wootton. Alas, the rain fell, spoiling the arches and making the bystanders cover their best clothes with cloaks and umbrellas. The splendid church gave sanctuary and beauty to the occasion. The couple later left Hollybank for a honeymoon tour to York, Durham and Scotland. There appears to be no photograph of this wedding. It is possible that the downpour prevented the guests grouping themselves.

The honeymoon over, Kilvert and Elizabeth returned to Wootton and they were in high spirits. A niece remembered Kilvert showing her grandmother in how many ways a Scottish plaid could be worn, parading up and down the drawing room. If we know comparatively little about the wedding at Wootton, we know much more of the homecoming to Bredwardine from the *Hereford Times* of Saturday 20th September 1879. On Saturday the 13th September the Kilverts returned to Bredwardine. Again rain fell heavily, but the paper tells us that it did not quench the warmth of the occasion. As in Wootton the village people erected arches, decorated poles and made nosegays spelling the inscription 'Welcome Home.'

> The first archway was erected at 'Church Town', the entrance of the drive from the high road to the church. There was a painting by a local genius and the decoration was by Miss Anne Leavis of Clappitts Cottage. The second was at the entrance to the Vicarage, and was erected under the instruction of the Misses Newton of The Cottage. The words 'Welcome Home' were enclosed on either side with the initials of the happy pair, all being wrought in ornamental letters and the whole structure decorated with bannerets.

Brobury too had triumphal arches of elegant design. "The first stood opposite the residence of Mr Williams of Brobury Court and bespoke much taste, pains and care: the second near the residence of Mr James Powell, coal agent etc., which was quite a model of good taste and construction being solely due to the exertions and industry of Miss J. Powell". One almost senses the reporters' reverence for rank, for praise for efforts is allied to it and the formidable Misses Newton are in a class all of their own.

Under the cedar trees tables were laid and tea was served to the school-children, then to the old women of the parish and last, "if they chose to partake sober minded-men". At five o'clock a band of labourers crossed the old bridge at Bredwardine and went towards Brobury where they shortly met the carriage of Kilvert and his bride. They were received with the waving of banners and hearty shouting. They crossed the river to the Bredwardine side and the horses were taken from the shafts; ropes were attached and amidst more cheering the Kilverts were pulled by human strength to their front door.

Mr Frank Weston for the tenant farmers provided and presented an illuminated address. Kilvert replied handsomely saying how touched he was, especially by the address. He thought "its intrinsic value very considerable". With it went a set of silver dessert spoons and forks and a caddy spoon. Then they were given another address and a pair of heavy silver table spoons in a morocco case by the cottagers. Kilvert replied:

> this touches me more deeply still, because I know it is given from slender incomes and pockets not very deep. This beautiful gift has, I believe, been prompted by a love which I feel I very little deserve [No, No]. But if God spares me I will try to deserve your affection and show you how deeply grateful I am.

# 20.

# The Last Irony

The triumphal entry of Francis and Elizabeth Kilvert into Bredwardine had been on Saturday 13th September. The following day Kilvert, following his usual custom, had services at Bredwardine and Brobury. In the evening he felt unwell and, no doubt, he and his bride felt that it was reaction to all the emotion and excitement of the previous day and the weeks before. His father was worried and he came over from Langley Burrell to do duty for him at Bredwardine on Sunday the 21st. He wished to set his son's mind at rest about the fulfilment of services. Andrew Pope, ever Kilvert's good friend, also came over from Preston to take the evening service in Brobury. He visited Kilvert that evening, and Kilvert told him that he would soon be better and up and about.

On the Monday he was not better and Dr Giles of Staunton telegraphed Dr Debenham of Presteigne to come and give a second opinion. Dr Giles was an able doctor and it is very probable that he knew that there was nothing he could do except hope. Twenty minutes after the second doctor had seen him Kilvert died. He had remained conscious until thirty seconds before he finally expired. He died of peritonitis; his appendix had burst. He must have endured great pain. He had seen many children suffering much sickness and distress die of the same complaint, which was commonly called inflammation of the bowels. The date was 23rd September 1879.

Only eight months later in the great city of Birmingham, some sixty miles away, Robert Lawson Tait performed the first deliberate appendicectomy for acute appendicitis at the Hospital for Diseases of Women. This was the first operation of its kind and the patient recovered. It was the beginning of a success story in surgery. Its growth in practice was gradual, gaining more ground as more effective anaesthetics were developed. In the late 1890s it had so proved itself that in 1902 Sir Frederick Treves (of Elephant Man fame) was able to operate on King Edward VII with every confidence of the outcome. He succeeded in making appendicitis a very fashionable complaint. Kilvert was removed from this surgery by a few months, and so removed from life.

The greatest shock of all was for the young bride. Her hopes and her happiness were dashed after a marriage of only five weeks. The family, Dora, Thersie, Emily and Fanny felt it all keenly too, but most of all Kilvert's father seemed utterly broken. He could continue no longer and when he returned to Langley he resigned the living.

The shock rippled out into the parish like little waves in a pond. The *Hereford Times* spoke of consternation throughout the neighbourhood and nearly all work was brought to a standstill. In what was admittedly a small close-knit parish this was no exaggeration. The present writer has seen, even a hundred years later, the tragic effect a young death in a vicarage can have upon a community. It is not just the sudden death, but a lingering belief that God does not permit such happenings to occur to those who serve him.

Early on the day of the funeral, Elizabeth Kilvert and Dora (now Pitcairn) went the few yards from the back of the rectory to the churchyard to decorate the grave with flowers. To their surprise they found that the task was already done, for the women of the village had flowered the grave. They left their flowers and Elizabeth, like the vicar's wife she had seemed destined to be, with Dora moved from group to group of the grieving women beneath the trees. It is a picture of grief and hope and great fortitude. Perhaps that was the true Kilvertian moment of the funeral rites; no set words, no ceremony, but tears, and flowers beneath the ancient trees.

The actual funeral took place in dark, gloomy mist with showers. It did little to help the unhappy people. Elizabeth Kilvert and her father John Rowland were the chief mourners. Kilvert's father and brother Edward and all his sisters were present. It seems his mother adhered to the older custom and did not attend. Often the congregations at funerals were composed of men while the women remained in the darkened house, supervising the 'bake meats'.

The Order of Foresters, so appropriate to Moccas nearby, paraded with their badges of office. At the churchyard gate Richard Lister Venables received for the last time his one time curate and ever friend. The local paper says how touchingly he conducted the first part of the service. Kilvert's clerical neighbours all took part in a very simple service containing no hymns. The children at the close put wreaths and flowers into the grave.

The following day Sir George Cornewall, Rector of Moccas and Lord of the Manor, preached a memorial sermon. To our eyes it is too theological, too impersonal and too long. It possibly pleased Kilvert's father, but in no way does it conjure up the memory of the shepherd of his flock to the people at Bredwardine. In the afternoon at evening service William Smith of Monnington preached on his late brother-in-law. One hopes this was more on the level of his hearers and addressed their hearts.

Like all clergy widows Elizabeth Kilvert found herself homeless, and she returned to her father's house at Wootton. But she was also much taken up with a sudden flood of duties. There were the wedding presents to be acknowledged and thanks for good wishes accompanying news of her husband's death, as well as replies to the letters of condolence. The log book of Bredwardine School has her letter transcribed into its pages:

The Vicarage
Bredwardine
October 27th 1879

My dear children
Mrs Bates has told me of your kind and loving subscription for giving a present to your late Vicar, Mr Kilvert. I want to thank you and anyone else who may have joined in it *very very* heartily. It would have given my beloved husband the greatest pleasure to have a remembrance from you. He would have valued it so much as a proof of your love to him. The kind and hearty welcome from you and all in the parish at our homecoming touched us both very much. I shall carry away with me very kind thoughts of the people in Herefordshire. Your beautiful present I shall always look upon as one of my treasures. It will often remind me of you all, and the kindness and consideration shown to me during these weeks of overwhelming and inexpressible sorrow.

Again thanking you all *very* very much
Believe me always
Your affectionate friend
Elizabeth Kilvert

She left the banks of the Wye which like so many things of intense beauty remain untouched by the rigours of this world and retain a great serenity. It is a serenity which is both strange and compelling to this day.

Another letter of this time came from Fanny Kilvert, and it was a cry to the heart to Mrs Venables who seemed to invite such confidences with her quick sympathy allied with such practical resolution.

Dear Mrs Venables
This is the first letter I have written since we came here (our new home) and I am writing to you first because I feel you can feel with us better than almost anyone in our great sorrow. I think sometimes can it be only 15 days since our darling left us — it seems many years ago. I have been longing to tell you some little things which I think perhaps no one else may have told you . . . I am glad for him that he is safe at home with 'Our Father' but I can't be glad for myself — he was so very much to me. Especially the last two years his tenderness and love seemed such a rock to rest on. On his wedding day his last look and word was for me. As he got into the carriage to go away 'Goodbye Fanny' they seem to echo and re-echo through my heart and to think that I shall never never hear him speak to me again on earth . . . . I feel very more and more sure how that he had been slowly passing away from us ever since his terrible sorrow. It just crushed him. I did so hope that his marriage would have cheered him and broken off all those sad remembrances and I believe he would have been very different — but his health was quite broken up — it is terrible to think of the sad cause of it all. I hope she will never know what she did. Poor Lizzie's letters are so sad and heart-breaking. Every day seems to make her feel her great loss. I like her and love her more than I can say . . .

It was presumed that the cause of Kilvert's depression and lowness of spirits was his love for Ettie Meredith Brown. Now we know that that love, though real, was from the start doomed. The greater blow was Katharine Heanley's rejection after acceptance. It should be remembered too that after Edward's marriage it was Fanny who accompanied her brother to the Hilton family in Faversham where they were all so heavy-hearted, for a reason not yet apparent.

This letter was written from the Kilverts' new home. This would be Beaufort East, a very pleasant terrace of Georgian houses in Bath with dignity and elegance of good proportions. Immediately behind the terrace is a church where one hopes the broken old man found consolation. He died in 1882 and was buried in Langley Burrell. The same quotation from the Epistle to the Hebrews is on his grave, but it rings with none of the vibrancy that it does on the grave in Bredwardine. Thermuthis, his wife, lived a few years longer. When her domestic ties and duties were done, Fanny entered the Anglican Order of St John the Baptist at Clewer and there she remained, content and hard working until her death in 1929.

Elizabeth in Wootton redoubled her care for the sick and needy, and it is good to know that she was appreciated. Yearly, she returned to Bredwardine to tend her husband's grave, and no doubt she saw that, as time went by, the Misses Newton occupied the spaces on either side of her husband's grave. The close proximity of these maiden ladies led to mild rumours of their having been in love with Kilvert. It could be true, for clergy are often targets for the affection of such women. However, no reliance can be placed upon such remours. Yet it does seem regrettable that Elizabeth, a wife for so short a while, was denied burial by his side. A space could and should have been kept for her. So Elizabeth lies in the new churchyard, across the lane on the southern side, and even there at the extreme corner.

One of her first actions when she recovered from the shock of Kilvert's death was to go through his poems. No doubt the manuscript he had sent to Longman's was easy to lay hands upon. Like his family she enjoyed his often moral and didactic poetry. The poems were printed privately be Edward C. Alden of Oxford in 1882 and there is a touching short biography speaking of his "intense delight in objects of nature" and his happy years in Clyro. Then less conventionally: "He possessed a happy faculty, and felt an increasing delight in teaching young children. There was something in his manner with them and in his way of speaking to them which had an attraction almost magnetic. It was so wherever he went. He was most tender in his ministrations to them in sickness and nothing touched him so deeply as officiating at the funeral of a little child".

They were still thinking in lines of sorrow and recalling Little Davie. One feels that this is as much the writing of Dora as Elizabeth. Dora knew so much better the details of his ministry. The books were given to friends and parishioners and many of them were affectionately inscribed by Elizabeth and Dora. They were treasured by the receivers but, like many such books, little read.

When did Elizabeth read the diaries? It is very easy to imagine her having a great reluctance at first to enter so intimately into the part of the life she had not known of the man she had married for so short a while. When she did she must have been moved to greater love for him, and must have sustained a few shocks. She would find his rapture and joy in the people and country around Clyro. She could feel for his love for Daisy Thomas, but it would seem remote to her. Not least, she will have read of his loves for Ettie Meredith Brown and Katharine Heanley, occuring at the same time.

As a potentially "ideal vicar's wife" she would have been gladdened by her husband's enthusiasm and love for his work. The out-of-character enunciations about striking miners would not have dismayed her. With her background she would have heard such Tory growlings before and known that they never came to anything. But she did react, and fiercely to Katharine's breaking of the engagement. Was she angered, or saddened? A.L. Le Quesne has suggested that her burden was a tragic one. She found herself to be the fourth choice of her husband. He thinks she saw herself as "the choice of desperation and advancing middle age" so that "a voice of inner bitterness may well have whispered in her ear".

I think if she felt bitterness she reserved it for Katharine. She may very well have seen herself as the saviour of her husband, and she may well have found another woman who hurt him severely, well-nigh unforgivable. But it must have been tempered with the knowledge that without that revocation her own brief happiness would not have been achieved.

There is one thing of which we can be certain; namely, that

Kilvert never wrote anything even faintly derogatory about her, or even slightly critical. That was his nature. The diary is one of love and generosity on the whole. The wonder is that, lacking venom or spite, it does not become anaemic. Elizabeth found nothing to cause her shame, or make her secretive, but she was a retiring woman who disliked seeing herself written about. By her censoring she removed a facet of Kilvert's character, and she removed all possibility of knowledge and understanding of the St Harmon year. It could be that she purged those pages after Katharine's almost certain suicide. That was an act that would have upset her, re-opening an old wound, but it would also have buttressed her opinion that Katharine, with her determination and obsessions, was not the wife for her husband. There is tragedy in Elizabeth Kilvert, but there was a consolation too. She was his widow, and widowhood in Victorian and Edwardian times bestowed a special distinction. Queen Victoria had elevated it into an Order.

The family of the Kilverts remained and remains. It would seem that they endured reverses like all families; but they retained their place amongst the professional middle-classes, and though Thersie was widowed, yet her poverty was not as great, or as hampering, as that of her brother at a crucial point in his life.

The young curate living amongst the affluent went rook shooting on 17th May 1871. He went with the jolly company of Mynors, Morrell, Trewellyn, Blissett and Mrs Gaston. He did not like it. He admired their skill and he even admired their weapons, but his heart was for "the helpless, innocent, unsuspecting birds". Those names mean no more than the birds they destroyed. Who knows of them now? But the poor young curate has carved his name to last for ever because he had a secret, the same love for nature that he shared with an Anglican clergyman, a Herefordshire man of the seventeenth century, Thomas Traherne. They shared a sense of wonder which Traherne summed up in a stanza of his own:

A Stranger here,
Strange things doth meet, strange Glory see,
Strange treasures lodg'd in this fair World appear,
Strange all and New to me:
But that they mine should be who Nothing was,
That strangest is of all; yet brought to pass.

(The Salutation.)

# Bibliography

*Selections from the Diary of the Rev. Francis Kilvert*, edited by William Plomer. First published by Jonathan Cape Ltd. in three volumes, (1938, 1939, 1940). Reprinted with index, 1961.

*The Diary of Francis Kilvert, April-June 1870*, edited by Kathleen Hughes and Dafydd Ifans. Published by the National Library of Wales.

*The Diary of Francis Kilvert*, June-July 1870, edited by Dafydd Ifans. Published by the National Library of Wales.

*Kilvert's Cornish Diary. Journal No.4, 1870 from July 19th to August 6th. Cornwall*, edited by Richard Maber and Angela Tregoning. Published by Alison Hodge, Penzance, 1989.

Richard Chenevix-Trench. *English Past and Present*, 1889.

Kenneth R. Clew. *Kilvert's Bredwardine*, 1970.

*Kilvert's Langley Burrell*, 1981.

Richard Holmes. *Footsteps*, Hodder and Stoughton, 1885.

Frederick Grice. *Francis Kilvert and his World*, Caliban Books. 1983.

Owain W. Jones. *Llysdinam and Newbridge*, reprinted from *The Brycheiniog*.

A.L.Le Quesne. *After Kilvert*, Oxford University Press, 1978.

John R.H. Moorman. *A History of the Church in England*, Adam & Charles Black, 1958.

William Plomer. *Collected Poems*, Jonathan Cape, 1973.

R.S. Thomas. *Poetry for Supper*, Rupert Hart-Davis, 1958.

William Wordsworth. *The Poems*, ed. Thomas Hutchinson, Oxford University Press, 1923.

Kilvert Society Publications.

*Kilvert's Kathleen Mavourneen*, Eva Farmery & R.B. Taylor, 1980.

*The Other Francis Kilvert*, Teresa Williams & Frederick Grice, 1982.

*Who's Who in Kilvert's Diary*, compiled by F. Grice, 1977.

*Kilvert and the Wordsworth Circle*, R.I. Morgan, 1972.

*Looking Backwards*, edited by C.T.O. Prosser, 1969.

*More Chapters from the Kilvert Saga*, edited by C.T.O. Prosser.

*The Solitary of Lanbedr-Painscastle*, edited by C.T.O. Prosser, 1967.

*A Kilvert Kinswoman*, Anne Mallinson, 1963.

*The Rev. R.F. Kilvert and the Visual Arts*, Rosalind Billingham, 1979.

# Publisher's Acknowledgements

Acknowledgements are due to the National Library of Wales for permission to publish photographs 1, 2, 4 , 5, 6, 7, 8, 9, 10, 11, 12, 13, 14, 15, 16, 17, 18, 19, 20, 21, and to the *Guardian* for photograph 22.

Also to Jonathan Cape Ltd for permission to print an extract from William Plomer's 'Angel Satyr' and to William Collins Ltd for permission to print 'Country Clergy' by R.S. Thomas, from *Poetry for Supper* (1958).

The family tree and the map of 'Kilvert Country' are the work and copyright of Eugene Fiske, of the Kilvert Gallery.

The cover painting of Kilvert is by Ken Hutchinson.